LOVERS

LOVERS
The Story of Two Men

Interviews with
PHILIP GEFTER & NEIL ALAN MARKS

By MICHAEL DENNENY

AVON
PUBLISHERS OF BARD, CAMELOT AND DISCUS BOOKS

Parts of LOVERS: THE STORY OF TWO MEN *originally appeared in*
CHRISTOPHER STREET *Magazine.*

Photograph pages 70 and 138 courtesy of Bob Howard.
Photograph page 146 courtesy of Rich Balzano.
Cover and frontispiece photograph courtesy of Tom Jenkins.

AVON BOOKS
A division of
The Hearst Corporation
959 Eighth Avenue
New York, New York 10019

COVER AND INTERIOR DESIGN: NORA SHEEHAN

I want to thank Charles Ortleb, the Publisher of *Christopher Street* Magazine, where a shorter version of this work first appeared, for his support, encouragement, and nerve in publishing this project to begin with.

M.D.

This book is dedicated to
Harold Rosenberg and May Tabak.
                    M.D.

Contents

Preface

THE original impulse behind this dual interview stemmed from the state I found myself in after three affairs ended "disastrously" within the same number of years. In this situation the mind has a tendency to play the game of "what if?", to endlessly replay the same themes like a record caught in a groove, idiotically repeating one line—a psychological state caught with numbing precision by Kate Millett in *Sita*. I had become a burden to my friends and tedious to myself when I met Philip and Neil, whose own love affair had "ended" some six months earlier. I became intrigued by the fact that they had an unusual photo-documentation of the two and a half years of their love affair and even more intrigued to find out whether the themes of discord which had plagued me were totally idiosyncratic or whether they were the particularized expression of difficulties inherent in gay love, or perhaps in the loving of any other person.

Using a selection of the photographs as a focus, I proceeded to interview each, separately, over a series of occasions; the hundreds of pages of transcript that resulted were then edited down to the present piece. These interviews were conducted under the pressure of strong and unresolved emotions, of late night hours slowly turning to dawn, of the urgent need to understand what had happened and why. In the printed interviews I have tried to maintain the surface texture and rhythm of those intimate talks—the confusion and circling around a topic, the pauses and sentence fragments, the contradictions and sudden flashes of insight—for it seemed to me that the living texture of speech was as significant as what was said. This meant running the risk that Philip and Neil would sound less literate and more confused than is usually the case with interviews that are cleaned up editorially, where people speak in whole sentences and even paragraphs. This risk seemed insignificant compared to the larger question of whether it was appropriate to make such utterly private matters public.

"All happy families resemble one another," said Tolstoy, "but each unhappy family is unhappy in its own way." And in this age of pop psychology and instant sociology, it is relevant to

13

remember that we read novels—stories of very particular individuals, not of the average person—and they are of some use to us. These are not interviews with a "representative gay couple," if such should exist; they concern two very definite individuals. Like most individuals they are quite unlike the rest of us. Whether their story can be of use to the rest of us is for the reader to decide.

For my own part, I feel gratitude and honest admiration for their willingness to share this picture of themselves—for it is not *their* picture; inevitably it is *my* vision of them and their relationship, and there is no way I can maintain that I was merely a disinterested observer. Since they entrusted their self-presentation to me, I want to caution the reader to avoid hasty judgments. Neil says somewhere that he believes we are all made up of very profound and very superficial motivations and hate to admit the superficial ones—a notion I agree with. These two have been willing to expose both their profound emotions and their superficial feelings; their honesty should give us pause.

It is trite to remark that gay relations are uncharted territory, that none of us knows what we are doing. The following interviews are an attempt by two men to understand what happened to them.

M.D.

PHILIP

O KAY, this is photograph 1. I guess at this point I had just come out, although I'd already slept with a lot of men. I'd just gotten my hair cut and adopted a certain "gay" look, or what I recognized as a gay look, at that time. This is 1973.

How old were you?

I was twenty-one; I was cherubic. Neil, when he met me—and this is what I looked like—thought I was the quintessential innocent youth. That was his impression of me. Like Tadzio in *Death in Venice*, in fact—that's the image he had.

Is that what you thought you looked like?

To some extent, although at that time my self-image was not such that I thought I was really attractive at all. Throughout the relationship, Neil lauded me and constantly told me how absolutely gorgeous I was. I had never known it at that point, and even today I don't trust it. But that was his impression of me. It was not my impression of myself. I thought I was rea-

1

sonably good-looking, and I was trying to mold my image to be like an Upper East Side gay—not even Upper East Side, a West Village gay. But that was only because it was the only thing I knew, in terms of the gay world, at the time.

Picture number 2 is Neil when I first met him . . . a week after I first met him. We met in a writing class at the New School. And Neil approached me. In fact, I spoke to Neil first. I knew that he was gay somehow. He was in the back of the room, and I saw him staring at me as I was leaving, and we walked downstairs, didn't say a word to each other, walked out into the street, and I knew he was following me; I knew he was looking at me; I knew he was gay. I don't know how I knew that. And I said, "How do you like the professor?" Then we started talking, went to a coffee shop on Christopher Street—I didn't know what Christopher Street was at that time. He said later he was testing me, to see if I were gay, and if I were picking up on what was happening all around us. I didn't. We sat in the coffee shop and after about twenty minutes he asked me if I was straight. And I said not exactly, and went into the whole history of what was happening to me at that point. I was seeing a woman who was living with a guy who was involved with another guy, and it was very sordid. I was not attracted to Neil . . . at that point.

You were not attracted to Neil?

Not physically. At all. I mean you can see this is what he looked like then. And you'll see, later on, what he became. I knew at that point that I had a certain fantasy-type man. He was dark, hairy—Neil *was* hairy, bodily hairy. But that didn't register at the time. So I wasn't attracted to him. He looked very different when I first met him than he looked throughout the relationship. He didn't have his beard. Because his hair was short, it was much lighter than it appears to be when it's longer. Anyway, he invited me to his apartment, not that night—I didn't want to go that night—but I guess a week later I went to his apartment. I wasn't attracted to him; I walked in and within five minutes he jumped on me. And I went through this whole

2

thing—I said, Wait a minute! What are you doing? What is this? I mean, I knew this was a sexual arrangement, but like . . . wait a minute. Like wait. Hang on. And obviously there was something operating. I was attracted to him on some level which didn't present itself to me as physical or sexual at all at that point.

And how old was Neil then?

Twenty-five. Our birthdays were coming up relatively soon. I turned twenty-two and then he turned twenty-six.

What does he look like to you in that picture?

He looks like he came out of the fifties. He looks like a sensitive child. Yeah, a sensitive child. He does look very natural in this picture, which I really liked. I guess I responded to that. But somehow when he spoke about life, his general philosophy was really incongruous with what he looked like. Because he really does look like he's out of the fifties in this picture. I couldn't relate to the incongruity. It's also interesting. This is an aside. This was me. [3] About three weeks after I met him I got my hair cut. That wasn't what I looked like when

3

he met me, that was after he met me. And he went through a period of about two months of not being very attracted to me because I looked ghastly at the time, incredibly different. I hated what I looked like at the time. I was looking for a job and I figured the only way I would get a job was to get my hair cut. And I looked very preppy, looked . . . very, very, very young: I looked about eighteen. Very clean, very asexual. I *felt* very asexual. No—I felt that I *looked* asexual.

How did Neil react?

He went with me to get my hair cut. I was freaking out and he was very very cool about it, didn't say a word, and he was very supportive after. We were walking down the street and I was looking in windows and freaking out because I couldn't relate to it at all. And he was saying, "It's all right, it'll grow back." Only two months later did he tell me that he couldn't stand it and that I had lost my attractiveness to him.

The fourth photograph was taken about a month or two months after I met him. His hair started to grow and he started to grow his beard. One thing I *was* attracted to about Neil was that, even though his hair was very short and he was shaving, he had this very thick stubble, and I liked that a lot. I'm very attracted to it, sexually. I guess I started really falling in love with Neil about a month and a half after I met him. I even remember the day, I remember the moment, I remember what happened and what happened to my feelings when I fell in love with him. And this is . . .

What was the day and what was the moment?

I'd say it was a month and a half after I met him. I was at his apartment, it was late afternoon. It was autumn, it was about this time of day . . . just about this time. December first, the end of November. I had come in from looking for a job. We were lying on the couch; I don't think we had made love but we were just lying in each other's arms. It was starting to get dark. There was a very beautiful light in the room. And all of a sudden I realized that his body felt absolutely . . . it was like the perfect answer to all my needs. It was warm . . . At that point I was very needy. His body felt perfect. It *was* perfect. It was furry, it was warm, it was . . . Mommy and Daddy. The embodiment of Mommy and Daddy. This was how I felt about it at that point. All of a sudden I had all these romantic fantasies of this being what it was like in London or Paris in 1920, you know, on an autumn day. I mean it was very literary, the whole mood of what was happening. And this is what it was like. And I fell, I literally fell, I felt myself sink, felt myself submitting to the feelings which were greater than the control I had over them. And I fell in love with him that day. We were just lying in each other's arms and kind of laughing and talking, and in fact, he was asking me how much I loved him. I was saying, "I can't tell you that, I don't know that, I don't know that I love you." And it was . . . like . . . right after that conversation that all this happened, this feeling emerged. I didn't tell him about it that day.

Right after that we went to the store to shop; he was going to make me a banana curry for dinner. And I was *real* impressed with the fact that he could make a banana curry. I'd never even *had* a banana curry. I'd never known anyone who had made one before. I guess that was a symbol to me, an aspect of his worldliness which I was also seduced by; he had traveled a great deal, seemed much more worldly and much more experienced than I was. I guess all these things . . . contributed to that moment. This picture [4] was taken at that time. His beard had started to grow, his general image was darker. You know, if one were to describe Neil, one would say he's dark, kind of

hairy. I was very sexually attracted to that. Around that time I started to have sexual fantasies about him when he wasn't around, masturbatory fantasies. He was beginning to look more and more like my ideal fantasy image. And it's hard for me to say which molded which . . . whether the ideal fantasy image was *a priori* and had existed before I met Neil, or if it was formulating as my relationship with Neil was formulating. Does that make sense? That distinction?

Yes.

Also this photograph is revealing in terms of certain symbols. It was taken in the steam and it's real cloudy and nebulous and he's almost an apparition, a kind of dark satanic apparition coming out of the steam and smoke. And that's sort of how I was feeling about him, too. My own feelings were very nebulous, confused, and this presence was emerging, in my feelings, this kind of dark, satanic presence, which was taking control of my feelings, or making me lose control of my feelings.

Was this picture taken after you realized you were in love with him?

Yeah. Very soon after. A week after, three days after . . . Throughout the relationship, Neil also had this metaphor about us together . . . he was Night and I was Day, and that he represented all that was dark and evil and mysterious and intriguing about the world, and I represented goodness and daylight and sunshine and all that. I resented the metaphor throughout the relationship, but I think I resented it because there was probably a lot of truth to it. Okay . . . [*long pause*]

As I'm talking about this, I have to say my anxiety level is rising. I'm sitting here sighing a lot, and words . . . if I were in a more comfortable situation . . . words would come much more easily and they're not. I'm finding it harder to get to real specifics in describing us. These photographs are summoning a lot of feelings that I shouldn't have put away [*laughter*] . . .

Did your parents know you were gay at this time?

They found out about a week after I moved into Neil's apartment. My mother was on assignment and was in New York for two days. We were having dinner at my aunt's house and she asked me if I could spend the next evening with her, go out to dinner or something. I explained that I had to go to my group meeting and she asked what that was, and I explained it was a consciousness-raising group where we all tried to share common experiences and understand our common victimization. When everyone left the table she asked what kind of people were in this group. I said there was a doctor and two professors, people like that. And she asked how old were they? I said the oldest was forty-two . . . and she looked at me and said, "Are you the youngest?" And I said, "Yes," and she said, "Are they all men in your group?" And I said, "Yes." And she looked at me quizzically and said, "Are they all right?" At that point I almost threw up and I said, "If you mean are they gay, yes, they're gay." And she—her look was one of astonishment, fear . . . panic. She told me it was a lie, that it was going to destroy my future . . .

What was a lie?

That I was homosexual. It's called negation. She totally negated it. She asked me if my roommate, who was Neil at that point, was gay . . . and I told her yes.

Had she met Neil?

She had not met Neil. She just knew that I had moved into an apartment with this roommate. At that point she said, "Daddy is going to come to New York and take you out of that apartment." Well . . . I burst out laughing. You know, she couldn't possibly believe that he could do that. Anyway, her reaction since then has been one of total negation of my sexuality.

What do your parents do?

My mother is a professional photographer, my father is an executive. They live in Florida. I grew up in Florida. They've had gay friends for as long as I can remember . . . And they are always Left on most issues, very liberal . . . I was shocked at their reaction . . . my mother's reaction. My father reacted differently. My father called me up later that evening after he received a frantic call from my mother announcing my homosexuality. He asked me if this was really true, and I told him yes. And he couldn't understand because of my history. I guess I had girlfriends in high school. I had brought a girl home from college one vacation. And they assumed I was perfectly heterosexual . . . I mean he couldn't understand it at all. He came to New York periodically after that, just on weekends, you know, having dinner with me and taking walks with me to find out more about homosexuality. Ironically enough—or it's ironic to me—it's my father who really took the interest in finding out, and as a result, we have a much closer relationship.

He's revealed things about his life and his marriage to my mother, things most fathers would not reveal to their sons, as a result of trying to find out more about who I am and why I have this . . . um . . . um . . . aberration, as my mother terms it. It's adhered our relationship, my father's and mine. Unfortunately he had to be the liaison between my mother and myself on this issue. That had a great effect on my relationship too . . . in terms of my never quite feeling like the relationship was sanctioned. Not so much culturally, but very personally. On some level my parents couldn't . . . my mother wouldn't even acknowledge the relationship.

Did either one of them ever meet Neil?

No. At one point they came to New York for a week. They come about three or four times a year. One time—this was about a year after I moved in—I told them I simply wouldn't see them unless they had lunch with us, to meet Neil. My father agreed. He agreed unwillingly—he told me he was uncomfortable about doing it but he felt it was very important for me, so he agreed to do it. My mother refused. So I told her that until she agreed to do it, I would not see them. And I didn't. The next time my father was in New York he was going to take Neil and me out to lunch but I got the flu [*laughter*] . . . so they

ultimately never met, and I guess I was as uncomfortable about
their meeting Neil as they were.

One time they went to an opening at the Museum of Modern
Art and I was invited to go to this opening too. A friend of mine
had another ticket and I decided that if my parents wouldn't
meet Neil, at least Neil could *see* my parents. So this friend
brought Neil to the opening. I was going there with my parents
and pointed them out to Neil and he followed them around for
about two hours, listening to their conversation.

Did Neil's parents ever meet you?

Yeah, his parents met me.

Did they know Neil was gay?

Yeah, they knew that Neil was gay. They had dealt with that
revelation when Neil was seventeen, and it took them about five
or six years to accept the reality that he was gay.

They met me and knew that I was Neil's lover; they invited
me to dinner on Friday nights at their home. I went to their
family seder . . . his mother used to call me up and wish me a
happy birthday . . . and . . . um . . . I guess my rapport with
Neil's mother . . . I guess the interaction had mostly to do with
my mother's reaction. I would tell her about my mother's reactions to my sexuality and she being . . . having great expertise in
coming to terms with Neil's sexuality, felt she was an authority
on how mothers should deal with their children—their son's
sexuality—homosexuality . . . so she would give me advice on
how to deal with my mother. That was pretty much what we
talked about. His father and I would have very civil exchanges,
very warm, very nice. We didn't talk much, but I felt like one of
the family; they were my in-laws.

**So did you feel a certain amount of sanction from his parents'
reception?**

To an extent. It's complicated to a point because Neil's parents never quite accepted Neil . . . as a person. They sort
of—it's as if they had given up on Neil and hence—you know,
they just accepted Neil as who he is—um, without their ulti-

mate support and approval. Because of that, it was easy for us to be who we were with his parents. And somehow I recognized that . . . I recognized there was a certain kind of sanction of our relationship that was not the same kind of sanction, or approval, I had been brought up to respect, I guess . . . God . . . [*laughter*]

It makes sense, though.

It does . . . You know Neil never lived up to his parents' expectations. They wanted him to be a businessman, have a nine-to-five job. Neil doesn't have the externals that parents can brag about. And I'm still locked into some of those prescriptions. You know, it's important for me to hold a respectable job; a job that . . .

Gives you public standing in the world?

It's not so much that . . . a job that means something in the world, a job where I could be creative and useful in some important way. In a broader sense, more on the cultural level than on an individual day-to-day bureaucratic level. My brother is a doctor, my sister is a lawyer. They're approved of by my parents. I'm approved of—to a point—in terms of my job now and in terms of what I ultimately want to do with my life.

Your job now being?

An editor in a photography publishing company. I work for a magazine, a quarterly of photography, and for a publisher of quite distinguished photography books.

Did you have any problems with the fact that while Neil also obviously needs to have creative, meaningful work, he doesn't need to have it socially sanctioned by any institutions, doesn't need the reassurance a nine-to-five job gives you about your place in the world?

Not at first. I have enormous respect for Neil as a writer, and Neil's ambition to become a writer. It started bothering me later on that he wasn't interested in the same cultural reference points that I'm interested in. For instance, I would be very impressed if he wrote essays in *The New York Review of Books* or the *Partisan Review*, or something like that. I guess I'm enamored with certain publications which are highly revered in academic communities and professional communities—intellectually respectable. Somehow if he had started writing for those kinds of publications I would have continued to admire his need and desire to write. Unfortunately Neil worked on two novels while we lived together, and worked earnestly and continually for a period of months. But after the first draft, four months or so, he'd give up and put it away. And eventually I started to realize that he didn't have the tenacity that I had initially admired . . . uh . . . I don't know if that answered the question. It didn't bother me in the sense that it would bother my parents if I didn't have a job with a name institution. I was brought up on those things in the world which are prestigious and by the virtue of that prestige they have some content. I realize that that's not true, most of the time; but, somewhere in the back of my brain, is my parents' indoctrination. I can't help but apply that to . . . Neil's writing . . . at this point.

Did you get exasperated because he didn't finish?

Yeah, I would get annoyed. Neil would complain that he was not doing any work, he would complain that he was not being published, and I would explain that he wasn't being published because he wasn't working hard enough at it, that he couldn't expect to write a novel in four months. He can't expect to write one draft and say it's finished . . . or even to have anybody read it, or want to read it. You know it takes a *lot* of work. And I started to see in Neil the desire to publish more than the desire to write, somehow . . . and I started to really fundamentally question what it was that was motivating him. I mean in terms of how he saw himself, who he thought he was, and whether there was some real validity in how he was billing himself.

How did you feel about Neil doing the gay radio show and being a personality in that particular, not quite respectable, subculture?

Well, I actually very much admired that not quite respectable subculture. I mean the sixties had a great effect on him. When Neil first started doing the radio show, I was *real* pleased. I thought it was a wonderful format for him to talk about a lot of his theories, a lot of his own experiences in the gay world. Somehow I thought that would be very helpful to people, and he had some very good ideas and made some very good connections in terms of songs and articles he's read and analyses he's made about gay culture. But eventually I started to see Neil enjoying the fact that he was a personality more than the fact that he was there on some kind of mission. And I saw the job as somehow being somewhat evangelical for the gay world. Not as a missionary, but as a spokesman, a spokesman about gay culture. Somehow Neil started to get off on his radio persona and started to trip out on the fact that he was this personality rather than someone who is there for and with the responsibility of the gay community in mind . . . It started to annoy me [*sigh—long pause*] . . . well . . .

Did you think he respected your work?

Yeah, I think he did. But I worked less than Neil, in terms of my own work, in terms of photographs and drawing, partly because I had a nine-to-five job.

How about the nine-to-five job? Did you think of that as a grubby way to make money or . . .

Well I thought I needed the job. I had to make money. But I also saw the job as the beginning of the ladder of my career, related to my career, which deals with photography. I worked at Time-Life, in the picture collection, researching photographs, editing photographs, looking at photographs . . . so I was connected to what I wanted to do. Still I was there eighty percent because I had to live, to eat, and, as long as I was making money, I thought I should make money at something which was going into my lifework. But it gave me very little time to do my own photography or to draw. I was also in graduate school, I went to NYU at night.

In what? Photography?

No, *comparative aesthetics*, which was a bit esoteric, abstruse. So, I was working nine to five—actually ten to five-thirty—and going to school two nights a week, and working very little at my own work. Neil had a great deal of faith in my talent. He believed I was really talented, but I was too young for him to take seriously. He could write off my lack of discipline because of my being young, in my early twenties, and just trying to get settled in the world.

Was his response to your photography useful, beneficial, stimulating—?

No, his response to my photography was very personal. Particularly given the fact that most of the photographs I took while I was living with him were *of* him. It was hard for him to have any real perspective on the photographs as *photographs.* Rather he viewed them as photographs of himself. And his criteria for looking at the photographs had more to do with whether or not he liked what he looked like and not whether or not he liked the images.

How about your response to his writing? Did you read what he was writing? I mean, there's a terrific parallel: at least one of Neil's novels was about you—as your photographs were of him.

Neil began that novel three or four months after I moved in. I would read the chapters as he was writing them, and I'd think I was giving him real critical perceptions about the writing—when in fact I was responding to me, the character "Philip" in his novel. Pretty much in the same way he was responding to my photographs of him. I'd talk about sentence structure or *pretend* to talk about sentence structure and all of that. What I was *really* talking about was that I didn't like how he portrayed me. Neither of us was a very good critic of the other's work, to be sure. A lot of that has to do with the fact that both of us were in each other's work. He wrote a novel about me, I photographed him. We were *very* taken with each other. [*laughter*]

You said Neil didn't have demanding standards about your work because he thought you were young, fooling around to some extent, not settled down. Did that ever bug you?

No. It was sort of an excuse I liked. As much as Neil accepted the fact that I was young and hadn't really settled down into my craft, I was going through constant frustration, turmoil, and guilt from not working as much as I thought I should. Part of my reaction to Neil not working as much as I thought he should had a lot to do with projection—it was a total projection of my own guilt. Absolutely. [*long pause*]

You want to go on to the next photo?

Okay . . . This photo [5] is probably the only photo I really love of me, a photo that Neil took. First off, I think it's a photo that looks more like me than any other. I also think it's a very flattering photograph. Of any of the pictures Neil has ever taken of me, it comes closest to what I think I look like. [*pause*] I guess when I said it's flattering I also think I'm pretty good-looking. And that picture sort of reinforces it. I also have to say, as an aside which is relevant, I printed this picture, and as I watched it emerge in the developer, the immediate flash feeling I had was that I wanted to fuck this person . . . who was me. (Heh) And . . . I didn't know what to do with that feeling. Like I didn't know just how to deal with it *at all*.

This picture was taken in the forest in Connecticut, where Neil and I spent a weekend. Someone Neil knew two years before called him up and invited him up for a *ménage* with him and his lover. And Neil said he had a lover too. The guy never met me but said he trusted Neil's taste, so the two of us should come up and spend the weekend in this house with these guys and have this wonderful *ménage* all weekend. So we went up. I was incredibly frightened by the whole thing. Neil and I had had a *ménage* six months earlier, which was a disaster. I freaked out during the first *ménage* primarily because the two people were more turned on to Neil than to me.

5

At the time of this picture, we had lived together for about six months. I was very frightened, I guess, because we were going under the aegis of this guy who had had sex with Neil two years before and really thought Neil was a hot fuck, right? So I knew this guy was very turned on to Neil. I also knew at this point in our relationship that Neil and I were very different types, and that we attracted very different kinds of people. And chances are, if this guy is real turned on to Neil, he would not really be turned on to me. Which means that I was putting myself in the position all over again of the *ménage* of six months earlier, in which I totally freaked out. [*laughter*] And started seeing a shrink—or I guess that was the catalyst for starting to see a shrink. So we went up to Connecticut, and I decided to do it just because I had to test myself. But it turned out the other guy, who had never met Neil, was very much turned on to me. And when we finally had . . . a sexual episode, we paired off—in the same bed, but the other guy, Bob, was with me and Frank was with Neil. And Bob and I got very into it. Neil got very threatened, ultimately, and the next morning— Neil and I slept in another bedroom—and the next morning when I woke, Neil was still sleeping, and I went to the other room and had sex with the guy again, then came back into our bedroom, and Neil had to have sex with me. And I see it all having to do with his being threatened. Later that morning we went out for a walk, and that's when this picture was taken. In the woods it was very, very idyllic, very romantic; it was a real rapprochement.

He didn't say anything about being upset?

Not until a few days later. He mentioned the fact that he was very threatened . . . And, okay, one of the things I was very pleased with is the revenge aspect on my part. I didn't know it would work out the way it did, but I was glad it did because I wanted Neil to know what it felt like to be that threatened. I wanted him to know what it felt like to be anxious, to fear that kind of loss, to be sexually threatened, to have his whole sexuality really tested . . . because I had felt that way six months earlier in the other foursome we had. And it gave Neil a lot of control over my head, and a lot of power, sexual power that I didn't feel I had. And in this foursome in Connecticut, it was the reverse. I had a lot of sexual power and I really liked that power and really needed that power. One of my general operatives in life is sexual; I see myself as very sexual, and for the first six months of our relationship I didn't feel that sexual power base. I was very, very, traumatized about that. Neil photographed me as this very Botticelliesque figure. And my theory about it is that, because he was so threatened, he had to create a fantasy or an illusion about me, and he was in love with the fantasy of me more than he was in love with me, or more than loving me. He also loves this picture of me. He adores it . . . The sexual dynamic of the relationship was that Neil couldn't be entered. I mean he had a very hard time relinquishing control, sexually. Neil's sexual dynamic is generally that he has to be in control. Neil's the first person who ever entered me and I really enjoyed it. I mean before that, two or three people had tried and I couldn't. I just couldn't let it happen. And Neil entered me the day after our first foursome when I needed him . . . I mean . . . I really felt threatened by the fact that he had been more attractive to the other people.

And when he entered me I guess I was really receptive and really needed him. I guess pretty much throughout the relationship Neil entered me and I have constructed all these dichotomies about what it means to be the penetrator or the fucker, like "he fucks someone over," or "he's getting fucked over." And I started to construct these hypotheses in my head. I started seeing myself as the person who was being fucked, and thus being fucked over. The implications are much broader in terms of constructing roles. I was the woman in the relationship and he was the man. And that entered my whole life and permeated my life in terms of how I saw myself. I started seeing myself as very feminine. I couldn't fuck, even when I went to the baths or to pick people up, I lost all my confidence and felt like I couldn't fuck as well as Neil could fuck me; in other words, I couldn't fuck, hence I just had to be fucked. And hence I lost my manliness, my masculinity; I became very feminine. I *felt* very feminine although I never really adopted feminine postures per se, nor came off as particularly feminine, but certainly that was my self-image for a long time. It was very destructive in terms of the relationship.

As I was feeling all these things, concurrently I also had a lot of political theories—gay political theories—which had to do with not operating from the road maps or guidelines of heterosexual relationships. I mean not having role definitions. We had to create and construct our own, which had nothing to do with male-female, dominant-passive patterns and all of that stuff,

having to do with a lot of heterosexually defined relationships. Yet I was operating from heterosexual patterns, constructing male-female operatives in the relationship, which
went against everything I was spouting. Which ultimately
ended up in making me very schizy throughout the relationship,
because emotionally I was operating on very different grounds
than my theory. Aside from that, I always saw Neil as much
more sexual than I, because I felt that I was very feminine and
I wasn't turned on to that. And since I was not what I was
turned on to, I felt like I wasn't sexual at all.

Although, when you saw the photograph . . .

. . . although when I saw the photograph I wanted to fuck
this person. Which created a dual feeling for me. I liked the
idea and hated the idea at the same time. Because it meant that
I was very fuckable, which meant that I was very feminine.
Which reinforced all the feelings that I had about myself, the
negative self-image. Yet I liked what I looked like, and I liked
the fact that I could attract somebody to fuck me. So I was very
schizy, to be sure.

**But you think this primarily came from Neil, this feminizing
of you?**

No, it came from me, but it came from my view of Neil. I
mean it ultimately did come from Neil, although I also did put
Neil into the role. But it was a role that Neil wanted to be in. I
don't know if I'm more responsible for it than Neil is, putting
himself in that role. Because Neil's image of himself is very
masculine—*very*—like he's the stud. Sees himself that way.
Very experienced; very worldly; very self-sufficient. He can
really take care of himself. This is Neil's image of himself.

But now part of the problem is that I resented that a lot
because, although I was very attracted to all those things in
Neil, and he was, in fact, many of those things, *I wasn't*, and I
knew I wasn't. I don't look like a stud. I mean I have a very
different look. I wasn't self-sufficient when I met him, I was
looking for a job, I was being supported by my parents. I didn't

know a lot of the things Neil knew; he knew a lot about the dynamics of the gay world I didn't know. He had studied in London, had traveled many places I hadn't been, stuff like that. All those things I wanted to catch up on; I wanted to be where he was. I wanted to feel that self-sufficiency, that self-containment; I wanted to be the stud. Because I was attracted to all that. And I have a "narcissism theory" about being attracted to all that I want to be. But I can't deal with the gap between what I want to be and what I am. I mean they're two different things. I think in fact at this point today I'm much more what I want to be than I have ever been, and closer to that ideal fantasy that I have, that Neil fulfilled. I'm also the age Neil was when he met me. I'm now twenty-five; he was twenty-five when I met him.

There was a lot of competition, of wanting to be what he was, which is because I wasn't there yet. The competition manifested itself throughout in seeing Neil as older than he was and his seeing me as younger than I was, and in terms of my seeing myself as more feminine and hating that.

Did you ever grow a beard?

A few months after I moved in, I started to grow a beard and I looked absolutely ridiculous. [*laughter*] I mean I looked absurd. I looked like I was trying to become Neil, and I felt like I wanted to become Neil. It made me real schizy. I mean, it just went against everything I am. I couldn't wear the beard; I just looked ridiculous. That's all. Looked like I was a fourteen-year-old child trying to look eighteen, or twenty.

Want to go on to Neil?

Yeah. This photograph [6] of Neil was taken the same time as the nude of me in Connecticut. Looking at this picture, and just seeing it as a stranger, it looks like someone who's really horrified, who's just in absolute shock. Knowing what's going on—the foursome in Connecticut, same context—I see Neil psychologically shaken up. He must be really threatened, and not posed there at all. I mean he really did curl his feet up as the cat walked by, and he's real scared . . . totally thrown off balance. And that's how I saw Neil at the time. Neil didn't talk about it; he became really introverted and real hostile to the guy who was attracted to me. That afternoon the three of us—not Neil, the other two and me—all went for a swim in a nearby stream. Neil refused to go. From that morning he wanted to leave. He couldn't take it. We had to take some late-afternoon bus or something. They were preparing dinner, but he just wanted to get out. He was very upset. But wouldn't talk about it until a couple of days later when he said he was threatened.

The next three pictures, I guess, visually summarize the three components of Neil I fell in love with or continually loved about Neil. This picture [7] shows a kind of resolute vulnerability which Neil didn't allow to come through very often. And victimized me as a result, because he wouldn't allow it to come through. One of the things I constructed in terms of the role I put Neil in was the fact that he was very self-sufficient and he wasn't very vulnerable. Although I knew it wasn't true, and I knew that somewhere he must be a real person with real feelings and real vulnerabilities, I didn't see it very often. I mean he wouldn't let it come through very often because he was reinforcing this role, this desired image he wanted me to have of him, 'cause he liked the image I had of him. All right. But one of the things I also remember was . . . Neil had a smile, the first month that I knew him, that was very . . . he never had that smile again. It was a smile of lack of assurance. It was a tentative smile. And it was the sort of thing I've never seen him do since . . . ever . . . I only remembered this recently. The smile. I'd forgotten about it for about two and a half years. The smile was his vulnerability. It was a half-smile and it was really tentative and it was real scared.

This picture to me reveals that same kind of vulnerability. It was only that vulnerability that allowed me to fall in love with him because I knew that he was a real person and that he *did* need me as much as I needed him. And I needed to know that. This picture was taken—in fact all three of these pictures were taken—on a trip to Provincetown. It was in the early fall, maybe a year after we met. And we were already living together for about nine months, ten months. Neil had an accident; he was hit by a car that August. He was in the hospital for about a week. I was really devastated by the fact that he was in the hospital; and every time he said he was in pain, tears would come to my eyes. He was very vulnerable at that point. This trip was in late September, a kind of recuperation, convalescence from the accident. And so he really needed me at that time. He couldn't walk around for long periods without getting dizzy; he was hit on his head and all that. This picture was taken at that time and he looks very vulnerable. I mean very real. It's a direct honest picture.

Most of the pictures I have of Neil are posed because Neil usually posed in front of the camera. Whenever I lifted the camera up to my face, he would immediately assume a pose.

But Neil enjoys poses, he enjoys doing that even without a camera being around.

Yes he does that without a camera. Part of Neil is posing. It's also the part I didn't like about him, even though I liked some of the postures . . . Okay, the picture of Neil. A vulnerable picture. It's sort of indicative to me of Neil the child, and in our relationship we did a lot of baby talk. We had our own language which we used to talk in. And we had pet names for each other. He was *Baby Ween* and I was *Ween Duck*. We had voices for these characters. We also had a menagerie of invisible animals and people that used to go to bed with us. (Heh Heh) It was very endearing in a lot of ways, and it was, I guess, one of the unique manifestations of our intimacy, in that it was *our* language and only *ours*, and we could have sex with other people, we could talk about everything with other people, but *that* was ours. It was something solely ours. And I saw Neil very

often as a child. Contrary to my whole image of him as a man, he was this little boy. I loved that image. Adored it. I also had certain theories about that, about the three-year-old *camaraderie*, like a new pure friendship; I don't know how to describe it. Very often I thought of us as little children, you know, who really loved each other in a real pure way and just played and had a good time with each other. And saw this image, had this image flash of Neil very often as a three-year-old kid and used to wonder very often what Neil had been like as a three-year-old. And I had little entertaining fantasies about what he must have been like. What they're about psychologically I'm not sure. But I loved it when we did our baby talk. This picture sort of represents to me the three-year-old Neil, at his most vulnerable, really needing me—that has a lot to do with it, I guess, really needing me. That's why I constructed those daydreams. I guess he didn't really need me very often. As the relationship progressed, we got more and more into talking baby talk to each other. And a lot of times we'd use that as the excuse *not* to deal with other things which should have been dealt with. It bordered on being psychotic, I think. He would call me at my office during office hours. I'd answer the phone and say hello and he'd answer me and say "Hi!" in his little baby talk kind of thing which I can't mimic. And I'd talk to him in a normal voice but I'd get off the phone and someone in the office would come up to ask a question and I'd say "Vat? Vat?" in *my* baby talk. It became a little strange. Just slightly out of control, I guess. But it was very endearing, it was very unique to our relationship. It was the *one* manifestation of intimacy. That's why I like that picture. Also, this picture is a reminder of Neil's hesitation with me at the beginning; the fact that he wanted me really badly and his smile was hesitant enough . . . and vulnerable enough . . . to make me realize or to make me see that. I don't ever talk about this . . . Christ . . . I guess I just needed that reminder, you know, that I meant a great deal to him and when he presented his vulnerability, it was a sign to me, an indication that he really did need me, and I needed to know that. He didn't communicate that as often as I needed it, and I guess I would have liked that. So I love that photograph for that reason.

[8] is Neil in front of the entrance to the house we stayed in. I guess in this picture Neil's posing. Definitely. I mean he's wearing a costume, a kind of thirties, twenties, Paris-literary costume like Proust, Pound, Hemingway . . .

Neil is very much fascinated by history . . . he studied history, and is very taken with literary history, and models himself after many historical figures. This photograph is representative of that, and of his general eccentricity . . . I see him as very eccentric. He has a lot of habits which I found fascinating and appealing, although they're not habits, more like hobbies. Things which I had no interest in, but I was fascinated by the fact that he was interested in them. For a period of time he collected old left-wing political buttons. He would walk around

8

the city to various stores and pawnshops and collect these buttons. And I was really intrigued by the endurance of his interest in this type of thing. He was really into it full force. That intrigued me in terms of his character, in terms of what made him the person he was.

He's also into collecting first editions of books and he's become very friendly with a number of book dealers in the city. He reads a great deal, and he reads things which I'm not particularly interested in reading although I recognize they're worthy things to read. He reads lots of biographies and I'm not interested in biography. But I'm impressed with the fact that he sustains interest in reading these biographies, and biographies about people I couldn't give a shit about, like Horace Greeley, Edith Sitwell, and Alma Mahler. What intrigues me is the fact he can do that, that he's interested in that. I guess all these things make him somewhat eccentric and hence somewhat glamorous to me. This picture really capsulizes it.

By eccentric do you mean bohemian intellectual?

To some extent . . . that's part of it. But that's not all of it. There are other eccentricities. He's a bohemian intellectual but also very aware of sociological processes and operatives in terms of the way the "real world" operates. He understands all of that and just simply rejects it . . . being on the periphery of society by choice, not just by the nature of who he is—he chooses that. And this picture sort of summarizes that for me.

Go on to the third?

Yes, the third is much heavier for me . . . Nine. This is the same trip to Provincetown. And this is Neil and I cruising. [*laughter*] . . . I guess this is the heaviest part of our relationship. I mean the heaviest in that it's the most unresolved and the most confusing for me and probably the most anxiety-provoking in terms of our mutual sexuality . . . who Neil was sexually out in the world and who I was sexually out in the world and who we were to each other sexually.

I guess my analysis of Neil's sexuality is such that he's permeated by guilt about it, and has created a character, a sexual character, and acts out of the role of that sexual character. A character who does not have a lot to do with who Neil really is, but who works very well in the sexual world. I mean he scores very well, etcetera . . . I also fell for the sexual character, which I could never reconcile. And I still can't. This picture capsulizes his half-Satanic, demonic quality, the world of mystery, of darkness, of night, of evil, which I am very turned on to sexually. The hunter. This is Neil's term, but it applies. I resented it for a long time. Neil is the hunter. And he'll get what he wants sexually. This photo reminds me of James Dean, Brando kinds of figures: leather jacket, a beard, strong look and those piercing eyes, *penetrating* eyes, darkness—taking a walk on the wild side. I think throughout our relationship I resented my attraction to him sexually. Totally resented it. Why? Because it presented to me the fact that I could never be that sexual paradigm, the kind of person I was attracted to.

What?

That I could never be that kind of person; I could never be a demonic, Satanic figure, sexually.

Why does that bother you?

Because I wanted to be. Because somehow . . . well, it had something to do with control and if one could control sexually, if one could make someone else submit sexually, apparently one had a certain control over oneself. I never felt that I had real control over myself. And here was Neil who could control me sexually, who could—I could get erections just by looking at him. I never felt I had that kind of power, that I could do that to anyone . . . that I could make them get erections, that I could lure them into bed, just by the nature of my being. And Neil could do that to me. And I resented it; I *hated* it. I also hated the control he had over me. I mean I despised that control he had. I *wanted* that control.

I wanted the same control over Neil as he had over me. All

right? And since I was attracted to that and that could control me, I mean that particular look, I wanted to *have* that kind of control. But I resented it, throughout the whole relationship. Despised it. [*laughter*] But loved it. It was a real dichotomy. It was schizy, to be sure. You know, 'cause I would lust after him and hate the fact that I was lusting after him. I also wanted to be lusted after; that was my big trip, to be lusted after.

How did Neil react to you, he didn't lust after you? He just said you were beautiful?

Right. Like my feeling is that he aesthetically adored me. *Aesthetically*. But that's very different from sexually. Even though I was the first person in his life he'd had any sustained sexual relationship with, he used to protest whenever I'd say "you're not really sexually attracted to me." He'd say, "that's not true. You're the only person I've ever had a sustained relationship with."

It's really complicated because Neil needs to be in control sexually, and when he loses control sexually he freaks out and can't function. He has to be in control, which means that he has to make the first moves sexually. It gets complicated by the fact that I could have sex about three times a day. I mean, I'm real hyper-sexed. And if I don't have sex I'll jerk off. Neil doesn't, he never jerks off.

Since I was always into having sex, and since I was lusting after him, I would initiate it a lot, which he hated. So I had to wait around until he wanted to have sex, which would be two to three times a week. That wasn't enough for me. I wanted more. So it caused a lot of problems. I would try to initiate sex more often and he would reject it. And whenever I was rejected sexually I would immediately think it meant he was not sexually attracted to me.

Did you ever try to initiate it by being seductive?

Yes. And occasionally it worked. Neil has a lot of energy. Amazing amounts of energy. But he's gonna burn himself out by the time he's forty. He wakes up in the morning and within five minutes he's up and he's ready to go out and run. He does a lot of things in the course of the day, and he invests a lot of energy in whatever he's doing. So, by the time I came home at night, he was already eighty percent burned out, just from doing whatever he was doing. Sometimes he had sex, very *often* he had sex during the day. That was the other thing. That was the *real* complication. I would get very pissed off and say, "you know, if you're not into having sex very often but you have sex outside, and if I'm not getting enough, how come you're having sex outside? You know, you're not satisfying me first. And you should meet your quota in the house before you can go out and do it."

If he could have sex with me once a day, then he could go out and have sex with other people. But he wasn't filling my quota, yet he was still having sex with other people. And I felt it was symptomatic of something in the relationship and if he was really . . . I mean this has all come out recently, after I moved out, that he was really scared of me sexually. He felt I had all this unleashed passion that he couldn't satisfy, and hence he felt out of control.

In addition, you pushed him into the position of being this big macho . . .

Well he loves that. He wanted that position. Although it was an expectation on him that was beyond his ability to feel comfortable with. Another problem was that I wanted to fuck him, too, and I really resented the roles that had been constructed. I understand it—I think I understand it—in terms of his psychic construct and why he can't relinquish control. And in terms of his not being able to be fucked by me—he never trusted me. He said from the beginning that he knew I was gonna leave him, and he felt that sometime I was gonna leave and he never trusted the fact that I was really there for him. And I understand . . . to a point . . . but I never believed that he really believed that, because I don't think I could have given of myself more to any person than I did to him.

Now the problem was always arising from the fact that I

never gave to him in ways that he *needed*, and I felt the same way about him: he never gave to me in ways that I really *needed*. Which is the ultimate destruction of the relationship, 'cause we just weren't satisfying each other's needs.

When he rejected me sexually, it meant two things simultaneously: one—he didn't really love me, and two—I was not sexually attractive. I mean that, that—there was a major problem [*laughter*], *to be sure*. It was *really* a major problem. Neil on the other hand had a very different sexual operative, which was that it was easier for him to have sex with people he didn't know. Also Neil constructs an illusion: the situation is equally important to him as the sexual act itself. If not more so. So that he can get off on dark streets, he can get off on seedy places, because they're sexual. He can get off on tea rooms, because of the situation, the environment. The environment is as sexual for him as the physical sensation. The quest is as important to him as the sexual act. To seduce somebody, to conquer somebody is almost as important, or *more* important, than what happens to get him to climax, physically.

And not for you?

Well, it's becoming more so, but not with Neil. With Neil, another reason it was hard for him to have sex when I initiated it was that I was already conquered. I mean there was no obstacle, it was no challenge. He couldn't go through the whole conquest, which I think is integral to what turns him on. He knew he *had* me, he knew I would have sex with him any time he wanted. And, you know, big deal. And I'm very different. Even now I don't like the conquest. Yes, I have to go through the seduction; yes, I have to meet somebody and talk to them and lure them into bed. But I would dispense with it if I could. If I had my druthers, I would just meet someone in bed rather than go through the whole process, the conquest. The seduction is intriguing. But that's not what really gets me off sexually. I'm much more interested in what happens physically, in tactile sensations, in looking at the person, both during the sexual act and before it.

What about photos [10] and [11]?

Philip cruising. [10]

10

You weren't really cruising, were you?

This is Provincetown.

Did you people cruise with cameras?

Yeah, sure. There was only one camera. We had to find somebody, and we didn't know if we were gonna find somebody to sleep with together or if each of us was gonna find somebody and go off with them. And I think that night we didn't find anybody, probably because I couldn't handle cruising with Neil. My identity, my autonomy was totally threatened. My confidence was threatened because of competition, which I talked about before—

Did you do this, normally, the two of you cruising together?

No. Neil always wanted to. And I didn't, I couldn't handle it. I always assumed that everyone was gonna be more turned on to him than to me . . . In this picture [10] I look like an innocent trying to be real tough. I guess that's what I look like there. A fourteen-year-old who has just seen a Brando movie and is walking around trying to carry off that image. But it's real clear, the disparity. The way I can tell is the position of the legs. They don't really look like they're firmly placed on the ground. Sort of from the basket up, I look tough and arrogant, although it's real hard to see my face in this. But even in the face, there's an arrogance to it. In the tilt of the head and the sway back of the shoulders, and the leaning against the wall. But again, this is more for Neil. Neil made me conscious of clothes. When I first met him, I used to wear loose jeans and sweatshirts. And he made me aware of the fact that clothes can be very sexual and can reveal one's body. I guess part of the reason I wore loose clothes was that I was not aware of my body at all. We were shopping and Neil liked this cap and thought I should buy it. [11] I liked it abstractly, but I didn't know if I would like it on me. I thought it was a nice cap as caps go, you know, but . . . I didn't think it was my image . . . at all. And although I sort of liked the way it looks on me, I realized it's not me and I was

uncomfortable wearing it because I knew when I took it off it fucked up my hair and that was somehow more important to me than what the cap looked like when I was wearing it. But I thought Neil wanted me to look like this. Neil loves that image. And that couldn't be further from who I am. I mean it's just . . . it's who I am when I feel real defensive. I know what I feel like when I do that. I don't like this picture, you know. I don't think it looks like me at all. At all.

Why?

I would not be attracted to that person. My criteria may be somewhat suspect, to be sure. However, I know I wouldn't be attracted to this person. Uh . . . I don't know. I mean I guess this is like . . . My feelings about these pictures with the cap basically have to do with the fact that *Neil* wanted me to look like this more than *I* wanted to look like this. Neil gave me lots of validation, like when I would wear a leather jacket. He loved the image. And I wore it more for him than for me. And I sort of felt trapped by that, too, because I wanted to attract him and wanted to keep him interested and wanted to satisfy him. His image of me. And I guess I resented that . . . It's called loss of identity, loss of autonomy, *loss of self*. That's how I see this picture now; that's how I would sum it up. A real manifestation of my loss of self—in the relationship.

Did you and Neil talk about what you looked like?

Yes. Yes. Neil said I was beautiful. He was always telling me how beautiful I was. He could never understand why I didn't see it. And I honestly didn't see it. I didn't feel sexual, I didn't feel beautiful. I felt like I was, um, reasonably good-looking, relatively speaking. But Neil really lauded my looks . . . he *lauded* them. Another reason I never quite trusted him is that I believed he thought I was good-looking, but *that* wasn't what was important to me. It was important that I was *sexual*. I mean, *fuck* being aesthetically pretty or good-looking. I wanted to be sexual. Neil doesn't have clean good looks, but he's very

very sexual. That was what was more important. I just felt Neil
was much more sexual because I was real attracted to him and
he didn't seem so attracted to me . . . It later comes out that
one of the reasons he didn't have sex with me as much as I
wanted was that he felt threatened—I seemed insatiable sexually. And I also used to do this number . . . we would have great
sex and I would *rhapsodize* right after it: oh how *terrific* that
was, and scream and yell at the climax and it was like real
heated and real exciting, but the next morning give him a list of
what was wrong with it. It was very fucked-up of me. He only
picked up on what I found wrong with it; he didn't pick up on
what I had displayed the night before . . . how wonderful it
was. Or he didn't understand the change, the immediate
change. And understandably. I resented the fact that I enjoyed
it so much, so the next morning I would indict him for it, for all
the things he didn't do absolutely perfectly . . . like not touching
me a certain way I wanted to be touched or something.

Let's go on to photo [12]

This was taken about two months before Neil and I went to
France for the summer. I wanted Neil to take a passport photo.
I was feeling real shitty that day; it was hot and muggy, I guess
in May, and nothing was going right. I remember that whole
day. I was real bored. And I decided I might as well do this
'cause we had to do it. So we were walking around SoHo, right
near our house, and I wasn't satisfied with any of the back-
grounds. I didn't want a brick wall and I didn't want graffiti on
the wall and I didn't want a parking lot and I didn't like anywhere. I was being real bitchy, real spoiled. Like a spoiled
little brat. And Neil was getting frustrated. He just wanted to
do it and get it over with. And there was no way I could find
the right spot. We used up half a roll. This is one of them. He
was saying "Come on, let's just do it." And I was really getting
furious, I mean *really* furious. I also know the anger had very
little to do with that immediate situation. It had to do with
other things, which I don't remember at this point. Probably
that we didn't have sex or something, or he had sex with some-

12

one else, or God knows what, but that was usually why I was
angry throughout the relationship. I have a theory related to
this picture, about love. Neil and my mother are the only two
people in the world I ever really get furious at. And I used to
get furious at Neil a lot . . . really vicious, vituperative, bitter,
screaming, yelling, really putting in the dagger. I can only do
that with him and my mother. This picture was one such occasion. I can see the fury in my face. Real hatred. I mean there's
hatred there. And one thing Neil could never understand is that
my anger was a sign of really strong feelings for him, I mean
incredibly strong feelings. He could never understand that anybody who loved anyone else could get angry at them. And I
have this theory: to love someone means to feel as many different kinds of feelings as strongly as possible for that person. The
full range of feelings. Which includes love, incredible need to
share, resentment, anger, tenderness, bitterness. I mean *everything*, the full gamut. I still believe this is so.

To love Neil wasn't just loving; it wasn't just sweetness and light and springtime and flowers. It was also real anger and real resentment and real jealousy and real bitterness. And real tenderness and real sharing and real caring and real loving. But he never understood that. He never accepted that. He never wanted to deal with that. He couldn't understand why I would get so angry with him. And he thought it was an act of hatred or dislike of him rather than a manifestation of the fact that I cared as much as I did.

You think Neil thought that love was some sort of benevolent, warm feeling.

Yeah. Right. Love was the fairy-tale versions of love . . . going off and living happily ever after. He didn't understand where the anger fit in. I think he started to, later on in the relationship, toward the end. It was very difficult for him to deal with my anger. I can understand that.

When I would exercise anger he would feel it was a betrayal of my love for him, rather than seeing it as part of my love for him. He also couldn't get angry at me and wouldn't get angry at me, and that would make me angry too. I saw that as an indication that he didn't really love me. For Neil, showing love was doing things *for* me: making dinner for me, going shopping for me, buying me things.

And for you?

For me, it was . . . being with him, holding him, talking to him, expressing it, talking about it. Also doing things. Like I started feeling really oppressed by the fact that Neil was able to do a lot of things. He was *able* to fix dinner; he was *able* to go shopping. He wrote at home. He didn't have a nine-to-five job. I did. So it was harder for me to do those kinds of things for him. And also out of anger or resentment at the fact that it was *his* way of showing me love, I would withhold just those things from him. And it was a real game. I realize more and more that it was a real game-playing kind of relationship. We did a lot of dances around each other. Like withholding a lot. Neil also, since he withheld sexually. I withheld in other ways. For me a really strong manifestation of love was to *make love* with him. But to Neil a strong manifestation was doing things, keeping the apartment clean, shopping, making dinner, things like that. He withheld from me sexually, I withheld in other ways. I wouldn't make dinner, I wouldn't go shopping. Things like that. It was a very clear tit for tat. As long as he's gonna withhold sexually, I'm gonna withhold from my responsibilities in other areas.

Another thing, in terms of anger, just as an example: we went to a party once in a giant loft not far from the house. And we had had sex just before we went to the party, at *my* instigation. I was almost begging him for it for over an hour. And finally we had sex. Neil wasn't into having sex; he was too exhausted, this was his excuse. Then we went to this party, and about an hour into the party he was off somewhere and I was talking to some guy who's coming on to me. All of a sudden Neil comes up to me and says, "There's this guy over there, he's like real hysterical, real hyper; he keeps coming on to me; I don't know what to do." And I said, "What do you want to do, Neil?" He said, "I don't know, I mean what should I do?" And he pointed the guy out to me. And I said "Um . . . it's real clear you want to go with him." And he said, "Yeah, but how do you feel about that?" And I said "Do whatever you want." I was *furious*. And so Neil left with this guy. And I *freaked*; I mean talk about anger, talk about despising somebody. I mean there was an active despising, hating, such fury. I wanted to kill him. I literally wanted to murder him. I had this fantasy. I left the party about five minutes after, hysterical—

Alone?

Alone. I walked the streets till three in the morning and I met somebody and it was the first night I ever slept out of the house all night. It turns out he made it with this guy in a car in about ten minutes and he went straight home. And I didn't come home all night, I was so furious. But I had all these murder fantasies. Fantasies of killing him off. I'd like to murder him, I'd like to beat the shit out of him, I'd take a gun and shoot him too.

I really wanted to murder him. It was an ultimate betrayal. And the thing is, I was in a CR group at the time; the next day I went to the CR group and I was really still hysterical. And I told them the story and everybody said, "Why didn't you say you didn't want him to go?" I mean it's the clearest thing. And—um—it never occurred to me. One of the reasons Neil did it was because I gave him this option to do it. I mean I said, "Do you want to go?" rather than saying, "Neil, I don't want you to do it." But I couldn't come out with "Neil, I don't want you to do it."

I expected Neil to know what was going on with me. But when I didn't know what was going on with him, I would use the fact that it's his responsibility to tell me. I would say, "Neil, I can't read your mind, you've got to tell me what's going on." But I would expect him to be able to read my mind.

You two were in separate CR groups and you didn't have friends in common before you met, but traveled in independent circles. How did that work once you got together?

I didn't see all of my old friends. I think each of us started seeing fewer of our previous friends. But there were a few on both sides we saw consistently throughout the relationship. They were privy to all of the ups and downs and crises, and knew the daily moods of our relationship.

Were they drawn from both Neil's friends and your friends?

Yeah, I would say so.

How did you socialize with your friends? Did you have dinner parties, did you meet them in gay bars?

Well, we both had straight friends. My two closest friends from before meeting Neil became Neil's and my close friends. They're married and have three children. I also had a very good friend from work, Susan. We'd have dinner either at their house or at our house, we'd go to movies together, or we'd go to concerts, or we'd all go dancing, late at night after a quiet dinner at our house or something like that. That's pretty much how we socialized with them.

How often?

Usually about twice a week, I would say, the two of us together. Neil also had his friends and I had my friends and we would spend separate evenings with them. He would go have dinner with a friend of his and I would go to a movie with a friend of mine.

But you never became one of these couples who were totally inseparable—you can't see one without seeing the other?

No, no. I would spend evenings with Susan alone over dinner, and then she would come to dinner at our house with the both of us. No, we didn't have to be seen together at all times. We were somewhat independent that way. I still felt jealousy when Neil went off with his friends, who were primarily gay—some of my friends were gay and some were not. Umm . . . most of Neil's friends were gay. And so I would feel a threat when he went off with his friends. And, in fact, I would go off with friends in order to compensate for my jealousy. I couldn't stay home and read while Neil went out—I would have to go out. We often didn't meet our friends in gay contexts, I guess. We would do other things with them. Although Neil and I were both very involved in a number of gay organizations and would go to their meetings, usually once or twice a week. You know these organizations, Gay Academic Union, Gay Activist Alliance, Gay Media Coalition—and out of these groups we did form a few friendships. And so we did meet in gay contexts . . . you know, after meetings we'd have coffee or a drink or something like that.

Do you think these friends provided you with any social validation as a couple?

The gay friends did, certainly, in that we were pretty much the only couple they knew [*laughter*] . . . or if not, the only couple they knew that lasted as long as we did, which was not all that long. But we seemed to have a permanent relationship, we had a home together, we shared our lives together, we were clearly very much involved with each other—and our friends set us up in the sense that we felt—like when I was going to move out, we felt like we were letting our small gay community down. The paragon was crumbling.

Did any of your friends not like Neil, or any of his friends not like you?

I think more of my friends didn't like Neil than Neil's friends didn't like me.

Was that a problem?

Yes, there was a problem . . . in that mostly I would deny that to Neil. It was certainly not a problem so much that they would not see me if Neil was there. They would see Neil. Most of my friends liked him though, or got along with him. We also used to use our friends a lot as sounding boards for our relationship and we would hold court with our friends as the jury, each of us giving our testimony about any particular incident during the week or the day before, rallying our friends' approval, so one of us could say to the other, "See, I told you so. See, I'm right." We spent a lot of time doing that at the expense of our friends and their needs and their desires. I think that was a mistake.

Do you think the validation you got as a couple from your friends was important to the relationship, as a sort of substitute for the lack of social validation?

Yeah, I do. I didn't get it from my parents and I didn't get it from people in my office. For example, my office held an annual picnic twice a year to which spouses were invited to come. The first two picnics I couldn't bring Neil, or I didn't know if I could bring Neil, so I didn't. I didn't feel the social sanction there, whereas our friends saw us as a couple very clearly. You know, somehow that served as an adherent for how we thought about ourselves. They provided support for the structure that we were trying to create for ourselves as a couple.

How about the gay world in general? Did that offer the same type of support? How did you relate to it? Did you go to bars?

No, we didn't go to bars together. I refused to go to bars with Neil; I refused to go cruising with Neil on the street. I didn't even like walking up Christopher Street with him. If we saw a film and we were walking home and Neil wanted to take a walk through the Village, I would not go with him. The gay world presented too much of a threat to our relationship, I felt—other than the political groups, where the people were related to each other not so much sexually but in theory and in analyses of the gay world, which was safer for me—the real gay world presented a sexual threat.

The gay world didn't seem very hospitable to a couple?

Right, absolutely.

I presume you never went to the baths together.

No, never. We went separately.

Fire Island?

Never.

Provincetown?

Provincetown we went to together, but we were staying in our straight friends' house, so it was a family situation.

That's very interesting; insofar as you were involved in the world, for instance at Time-Life, you weren't being seen as a couple. And the gay world made no room for you as a couple.

It could have, but I was too frightened. I mean I think the gay world exists in a way where couples do make themselves known as couples, and will cruise together and pick people up to take them home and they remain a couple and have threesomes. I simply never felt comfortable with that. I never felt comfortable as a couple in a sexual context. And gay contexts are primarily sexual contexts. Other than political groups.

Do you really think the gay context is primarily sexual?

Yes I do.

You don't think there is a certain society?

There is a certain society—it's a highly decadent society. The reason Fire Island exists, for instance, is because of the sexual operative which exists within that society, within that professional, upwardly mobile society of gay men. Well, yes, there are other interests than sexual interests, but if the sex weren't there or if sex weren't presented the way it is, then it would not be a gay context. It would not be a gay community.

Fire Island Pines is a very beautiful place, a very nice environment, but gay people have congregated there *because* there exists a sexual operative. They have also created the sexual operative because of the fact that they are a gay community. I don't know how to explain it. You can take anything which is stereotypically a gay interest—the opera, the theater. Gay people can come together in those contexts. They can meet at the opera, a museum opening, but they're not going to talk about sex. They won't overtly come on to each other sexually because of the context, the nature of that context is not gay. It is simply a cultural context.

The ballet world, the opera world, they're *not* predominantly gay; there are many, many gay people in those worlds, to be sure, but the principles of those worlds, if you look at them, are very heterosexually defined. Look at the opera; look at the ballet; they always deal with the man and the woman. Even the parties that they attend afterwards. Although everybody acknowledges the fact that eighty percent of the people there may be gay, you certainly couldn't see it from being an outsider looking at that party. It would look like any cocktail party in Westchester.

You're saying that the gay world, the gay culture insofar as it exists as a reality, is predominately a sexual creation.

Yes.

That is, its base is principally sexual?

Yes.

Interesting.

When Neil and I went to the opera or to a museum opening, or a straight cocktail party, I didn't feel threatened at all. In fact, I felt less threatened in those contexts than I felt as a couple in the gay community, because there was no basic threat to our relationship in those contexts. If anything we were real allies in those contexts.

Do you think that your perception of this is colored by the fact that you live in New York?

That may be true; I really don't know. It makes sense that it may just be in New York City, in that in New York City people find friends and discover their own milieu in terms of their own interests rather than their sexual proclivities, because there's always that availability later on in the evening of going out in pursuit of the satisfaction of your sexual needs, whereas in smaller towns all gay people have is each other because there aren't that many of them. And it turns out that gay people share interests in smaller communities.

Go on to the next photos?

These [13 and 14] were taken in Cannes. Neil and I had spent a month driving through France. We rented a car and camped out half the time, which got to be awfully uncomfortable. We realized we were much more bourgeois than we had ever considered. We went to Cannes for a week. I mean it was a *lovely* week. We had this lovely hotel, very cheap, breakfast in bed, and we'd wake up at eight o'clock and have croissants and coffee and drive to the beach, spend the whole day at the beach right outside of Cannes. It was a gay beach, it was a nude beach, it was not very crowded, and we just had this lovely day, every day, hanging out on the beach, reading and drawing and playing Scrabble with each other and talking, and each of us going off and cruising and we'd get off with other people where neither of us could see the other. For some reason

Cannes was the only place and the only time throughout our whole relationship that I was not really jealous. And at night, I think two or three different nights, we went separately with other people and had sex with them, and it was really fine. And I don't know why.

Did you have sex with each other?

Yeah, we had sex with each other. And that was good.

14

And you were being very successful when you went out by yourself?

Yes, absolutely. In fact at one point, I met this one guy, Bob, who lived in Cannes. And I was walking on the promenade with him and ran into Neil. And Neil saw this guy I was with and said, "He's gorgeous, I mean like I'm jealous but I can't not let you go home with him, he's so beautiful." And so Neil left so

I could go home with this guy because he thought, like wow, what a conquest. And I would never do that. I mean I know if I saw Neil with somebody who was that beautiful, I would freak out.

Even at this time?

Well, at this time, I don't know if I would be as threatened as I had been in the past, but I don't know if I could have been as gracious about it as Neil was. I was amazed at Neil's graciousness. But that was pretty much the way it was at Cannes: I mean it was just idyllic, lovely. And for me that week was the honeymoon. Two years after the fact. It was like *the* honeymoon.

What about picture [13]?

To me, this picture is Neil. It's a very private moment of Neil for me. We've just come back from the beach and I'm about to take a nap and Neil is already taking his nap. The two of us in this hotel room. It's a very intimate moment. I mean Neil is totally vulnerable; he's asleep, his back . . . like I'm behind him. His little tush is there. I mean he's very vulnerable. There's a part of this picture which is the three-year-old Neil, which I talked about before. Like he's mine. He's mine. Like we take care of each other. He can be vulnerable, he can lie there naked, asleep, with his back to me. In this most beautiful little room with late afternoon light.

In terms of this picture of me [14], I was seeing myself as looking very French. And I was very successful in France. I was a real hit, and I started seeing myself that way. Or feeling that way about myself. I took this picture, and you can see the difference, I think, between most of the pictures Neil took of me and this picture I took of myself.

My face looks totally different. My hair was also longer. I was also very tanned. And I felt real good about the way I looked. I was just playing in front of a mirror. I loved what I looked like. I also don't think I really look like this, but I guess there are times when I feel I do project this, this image, which is very French.

Whose idea was it to go to France?

Mine. I definitely wanted to take a full month's vacation, and I didn't do that the year before. And I decided I wanted to go to France and drive around the countryside. It was going to be my great romantic vacation. But my initial decision to go to France hadn't included Neil. I was going to go to France whether Neil went or not. We didn't know if Neil could afford it, and then we started talking about going together. So it was totally my initiation.

Right after Cannes we drove back to Paris. We were going to spend three days in Paris before I had to fly back to New York and Neil was going to drive off to Portugal. In Paris we spent one day and we were *miserable* with each other. We just found each other tedious and annoying. I wanted to go to museums and Neil just wanted to hang out, he didn't want to see museums. It was hot and we were coming down from this trip and we knew we were going to be separated for a month, so Neil decided he was going to leave. Just drive off to Portugal the next morning, and I was going to stay in Paris another two days. And when Neil suggested that, I said fine. *Terrific.* I had a friend who was staying in Paris, and I ended up staying with that friend for two days. But I was glad to get rid of Neil, and he was glad to go because we were *not* getting along at all. It was a real come-down after Cannes. So he drove me to Gare du Nord because I had to buy a ticket or something at the airport, and from there Neil drove off. Up till then I had driven the whole trip 'cause Neil didn't know how to drive standard transmission. I had to teach him while we were in France, but he'd get very frustrated 'cause it was taking him so long. He was not very adept at driving as he drove off, and he stalled out about five times in Paris traffic. I don't know if you've been to Paris, but he had to drive around the Arc de Triomphe, which is just insane. And my heart was in my mouth. Literally I felt like: I'm a father watching my son drive off for the first time, not really knowing how to drive, and I thought he was going to kill himself. I was really upset and worried about him. And that's how he departed for that month.

It's an interesting reversal.

Yes. It is a reversal, where I became the expert and assumed responsibility. I had an excellent sense of direction and assumed a lot of responsibility. I was deciding which way we would go—so I was coming into my own a lot. Even during that month in France. Out of the context of our daily lives I found I was much more confident about doing things than Neil was, about going to different places and judging situations. And jumping into situations. So I felt real good about it. And I guess that may have been catalytic in some ways in terms of our separation, in terms of my feeling self-contained enough and sure enough of myself to be able to leave Neil. That's not the only reason I left; I left for a lot of reasons.

But it sounds like the need was ebbing.

The need, right, I was always very needy and defined myself totally by Neil until that time. I like this picture [15] of me a

15

lot. This is much more my image of myself. I don't like the white robe but I do like the face. And I do like the blackness all around, the kind of slightly mysterious, intriguing element and that's more how I see myself.

First what was the setting, when this picture was taken?

Oh, we had either just had sex or were going to have sex. It was taken from our bed, which was above, on a loft. And I was sitting on a little couch right below the bed. I don't remember exactly what was going on; I'm not real clear about that. It had to be in the summertime, right after we came back from France. Right. What was going on at that point: Neil and I had been away from each other for a month. It was the first time we had ever spent a month apart. Virtually the first time we'd ever been apart. And it was the first time I'd lived in the apartment for a month alone, feeling like it was my apartment, which was another whole aspect of our relationship too. I never felt like it was my apartment. I moved into Neil's apartment and the whole time I lived there it was more Neil's apartment than mine.

How long had you been together?

Almost two years. I had sort of come into my own a lot that month. I was very much more self-contained than I ever had been in the relationship, because we'd been apart and I'd had a good time while Neil was away, although I missed him a lot the last week or two.

Were you playing around?

Yeah. I had a good deal of sex. I went to Fire Island one weekend with some guy and I was infatuated with someone else, a brief three-day infatuation. It was summer and I didn't work all the time. It was nice. But I was glad to see Neil when he got back. And this is soon after he got back.

Neil's money was just about gone, what with this trip to Portugal. And I was starting to support him; that was for only a month because he didn't have any money, and had to find a job.

So he started looking for a job, but he felt after about two or three weeks that I was using money as a control, as a heavy control.

Were you?

Not really . . . To an extent, but only to an extent. I mean we sat down one day and I said, "Neil, you're not gonna starve. Don't worry, I mean I've got money, I'm making money, I'll support you until you get a job." And it worked out all right for about two or three weeks: I gave him an allowance and I paid for all the domestics. I was feeling very weird in that position; I didn't like the position, particularly.

Not at all?

But Neil got very freaked out by it. He *hated* the fact that he had to ask me for money. He didn't know how to say "Philip, I need ten dollars." And so he would manifest it in various ways. He'd be real nasty to me, and it would come out two days later that he wanted to ask for money but didn't know how and was trying to cover up his need to ask for money. He was like that. This was all going on when he took this picture. But I think this picture is much more sympathetic than a lot of the other pictures he took. It's also interesting that he's looking down at me, and I'm the one who's supporting him. This time. I look like a child, very childlike in this. But also very seductive. I'm also looking up to him, in this picture. He lost a lot of his self-respect at that time.

Because he couldn't support himself?

Because he couldn't support himself. I also started getting angry at him after a month, or annoyed with him, because he wasn't actively looking for a job as much as one *should* in that situation. He would go on maybe one or two job interviews a week. I also realize it was very difficult for him. Neil only worked in the real world five months in his life. At Appleton-Century-Crofts. That was the extent of his work life. Everything else, any money he made was from free-lancing or his writing. Which is another aspect of the relationship I resented: that I had to go to work every day, and he didn't have to. And that presented a number of logistical problems and resentments throughout the relationship. After a month or so, he wasn't relying on me financially. A month after that, I started to feel an incredible indifference in the relationship. And that began the process which took about six months until I moved out.

Who was feeling the indifference? You or him?

I was. I was. Actively, I was. I was going through a lot of transitions, internal transitions. I started hating my job; really wanting to change my job, looking for other jobs. Feeling very uncomfortable about where I was: I had just become twenty-four, and was beginning to realize that I had to start doing something, directing myself toward a real career and a real goal and a real purpose, etcetera. I had a good job as a photo editor and researcher. But it wasn't what I wanted to do. I wasn't satisfied with myself, and I wasn't using my own creative resources. I was relying on the aegis of the corporation for my definition, and I was feeling very uncomfortable about that. So I was starting to want change, to make certain choices for myself, and it was around that time that I started paying less and less attention to Neil and the relationship and caring less and less about it. And Neil at that point started to care more and more about it and would periodically say to me: "Philip, what's going on? I don't know you anymore. I don't know where you are. What's happening? We're not talking."

I used to talk a lot. I used to demand a lot from Neil. I mean throughout the relationship, demand that he talk about what was going on. We would have marathon sessions about three or four times a week. Hours at the kitchen table about "What is going on? What are you feeling? What did you do today? Why are you feeling that way? Why did you do this thing yesterday? Let's talk about it." *Hours*. And he would hate it, but he would need it and love it. I mean ultimately. He was glad that I did that. Then he started becoming the one who was doing that. And I stopped talking a lot. He didn't know where I was. I was there but I wasn't there. And he would say, "You're not there; you're just not there." And it was true, I wasn't there. I guess this picture was taken just before this began.

I remember: we'd just had breakfast. He came in and sat down across from me and just looked at me. I looked up and I said, "What's the matter?" And he said, "I need reassurance from you." And I said "About what?" And he said, "That you're not gonna leave." And I hadn't actually actively thought about moving out, yet, but I was wondering if Neil was the right person for me. Or do I want to be in a relationship? And this stuff had sort of passed through my head, but I wasn't really consciously thinking of moving out. And Neil said this and I got really upset, not because he was upset; I got upset because I couldn't reassure him. And I think all I said to him was, "Don't worry; I'm not going to move out."

And about a month after that particular incident, he again said, "You know, you've got to tell me what's going on. You haven't been here in three months. I don't know what's going on, what you're thinking about, where you are, who you are, blah blah." And that's when I started talking to him about the fact that maybe we're not right for each other. What I had felt for these three months was more indifference than I had ever felt. I mean I wasn't totally indifferent, but I was not very concerned about the relationship.

And I had also met this guy that I started tricking with. It was the first person throughout my entire relationship with Neil that I saw more than once. And I started seeing him about once a week. And he's also the first person I never mentioned to Neil. It was very clear to me the second time I saw this guy—in fact, I actively lied to Neil about where I was going—I knew something was up. I mean something was up in my relationship with Neil that was really crucial. The need for having this father around was subsiding to some extent. I mean I was fairly responsible in life, and like I was gonna survive real well, without Neil. That presented itself.

Do you want to talk about [16]?

Right. Yeah. The one that Bob Howard took of me. This was taken in April, about two weeks before I actually moved out. A *lot* was going on here. Neil had jumped into a relationship with someone else, a month after I told him I was moving out, and I saw it as Neil's bait to try to get me back, and it worked to some extent, because I was feeling insanely jealous. I mean I'm the one who was moving out, but I couldn't deal with Neil

being involved with anyone else. And when this picture was taken I was probably at my worst. I'd just left my job, given up my security, I had just quit therapy, and I was moving out.

Growing up?

Interestingly enough, I started all those three things at the same time too: I moved in with Neil, started therapy, began a job at Time-Life within two weeks. And I continued those three for almost three years, and at this time, stopped all the three things at once. I mean I was literally coming apart. I was on Valium every day. I could not function. I would stay in bed but couldn't sleep; I would just walk around for hours, freaking out, crying a lot, really feeling anxious and walking around shaking most of the time. For a good month or so when this picture was taken. This picture is such an incredible anomaly to me. This was probably the worst day of my life, and yet I looked very self-contained, and content and fairly happy with myself and life. And yet I was abysmally unhappy. [*long pause*]

How do you think gay relationships differ from straight relationships?

. . . I think primarily in terms of the accessibility of sex in the gay world, and the fact that a lot of problems or conflicts which may appear in the relationship are easily acted out, outside of the relationship. It was very easy for me to get mad at Neil and say, "I'm going out tonight." I could go out and know that within two or three hours I could meet somebody and "contract" to have sex with him. I mean there's this operative in the gay world where two men can come together sexually, only sexually, and both of them know that that's the only reason. And if it's good sex they'll get the phone numbers and meet again. The straight world doesn't have that option, not quite as easily, anyway. It's a little bit more difficult for a straight man to step out of his apartment and know that he's going to find the momentary solution to his conflict. And within three hours in the gay world it's very easy.

How about the fact that gay people do not have children? And they don't have the validation—

Right, they don't have the externals imposed by the institution of marriage. They don't have the institutions to adhere their relationship. They don't have the in-laws; they don't have the children; they don't have the PTA; they don't have the office parties. It's got to come totally from within; it's got to come totally from within the relationship and it's got to come out of some real need and commitment and love, whereas a heterosexual couple who have been together for twenty years— I'm sure a lot of what they consider when they consider possibly parting is how they are going to tell the children, how they're going to make the break in their community of other couples who abide by that institution. They're going to have to deal with the alimony. They're going to have to deal with all the legal ramifications of being married and severing their ties. All of these things, you know, are great supports for those couples, those straight couples, to try to keep their marriage together. You know, gay people don't have that, none of those institutional supports to back them up. So it's got to come out of some real need, some real commitment to each other to try to keep it together and to try to remain allies against what is ultimately a hostile world to them.

So it sounds like the only thing to keep the gay couple together is either passion or comfort.

Passion *and* comfort. Yeah. I guess it's true. Also real love and respect. I don't think just passion and comfort. I think some kind of genuine respect for each other as well. And a relationship out of which self-growth can really occur; a relationship which fosters a growth of the two individuals by each other. I don't think it's just passion and comfort. It's a number of things really holding them together. But the two people have to be very strong in order to withstand all the pressures for them not being together. I mean there's got to be some very powerful motivation on the part of two gay men to sustain a relationship [*long pause*] . . . Ask me a question. I don't know what to say when you don't ask me questions.

The last bit interests me a lot. I'm just wondering whether it's feasible to build any kind of structure, you know, a personal structure that would last in time, on emotions. It seems to me that's an obvious reason why so many gays buy brownstones or summer houses or start businesses together.

Exactly, to provide their own institutional support, some kind of secure base, an economic and social commitment that the two of them share; I think that's very true. I also believe that we have the capacity to sustain an emotion once we are in touch with what we want in life.

You make it sound so easy: Once we are in touch with what we want. What do you want in life?

What do I want in life?

What is the most important thing that a lover could give to you? Or that Neil did give to you?

Respect. Nurturing my own work, fostering ideas, loving me. What does that mean? Loving me. Caring about those things that I cared about in ways that I cared about them.

Do you think you've gotten anything or do you get anything out of what we call the gay world besides that?

Sure.

Any type of validation or any type of—

Me personally?

You personally.

I get a lot of physical validation. It also depends on which level of the gay world you're referring to. I mean there's that level of the gay world which is connected to the arts. On that level of the gay world, oh, I don't know. Not necessarily. I mean I don't know if I get anything really from the gay world other than a sexual validation, a physical validation. I think there exists a sense of humor in the gay world that doesn't exist in straight heterosexual society, and a lot of that stems from the lack of responsibility gay men have. There is a certain cavalier level on which gay men can live their lives. They can still maintain their responsibility on their jobs and they can still be committed to their work; yet they don't have the children and they don't have the two or three homes. Again they don't have to answer to those external, societal, institutional supports.

Well, also the having of two lives may contribute a lot to the habit of irony.

That's true, absolutely.

Okay. I want to try to get you to encapsulate the whole relationship. This is three years out of your life.

Well, one thing I can say is that it provided probably the most existential arena for me to understand a lot about who I am. I don't know if that says anything. Things became real clear to me, I mean about myself, more in this arena than any other I've ever been in, I guess, in life. In terms of the way my feelings are constructed, the way my psychic construction operates, in terms of my own limitations and in terms of my potential, in a lot of different ways. I saw a lot of things about myself through this relationship with Neil.

You sound like you're saying you grew up . . .

Yeah, right, becoming more who I'm going to be because of this relationship. You could also say the relationship isn't over. I mean we don't know where we are. But it's not over because there are still incredibly strong feelings and we see each other often, talk to each other almost every day. Our lives are very much intertwined. We don't know how to define it, but we're also very much a part of each other. And I can't envision a time in my life when Neil won't be part of it. But in what context I don't know . . . I mean I think I did grow up to some extent. I mean I'm not grown up. I'm not the person I will be. But I'm well on the way. And the relationship is like *the* prime catalyst, more than anything else . . . It was also sort of destructive.

How? It seems you came out of it very well.

Except certain things are hindered, like my sexuality, the way I operate sexually.

Is hindered now?

Is hindered now. I mean I can fuck, I can get fucked. I can be real flexible, but I can't get emotionally involved.

How many months has it been—six?—not such a long time.

No, I know. There are certain people I see regularly at this point. Sexually. I told you that. Anytime they make any protestation of any feeling, I sexually withdraw. That is somewhat detrimental, I think.

I'm curious. What do you think you're looking for, in the person you'll next be involved with?

At this point I don't think anyone younger. At this point it would be older. I don't trust *young*. [*laughter*] I mean witness myself. I do *not* trust *young*. Neil and I should have met now, at this age. I mean he should have met me when I was twenty-five, not when I was twenty-one. There were too many things I had to go through . . . and I was *much* too needy. And he was too young to know how to satisfy those needs too, or know how to deal with them. Because he was still needy enough when he met me. The thing I see about our relationship, it was a failure in that we were emotionally too young.

Why do you say failure?

Because I moved out.

So any relationship that you don't stay together until one or the other dies is a failure?

Um . . . no, it has more to do with the reasons why I moved out, which was to reestablish my autonomy, myself, to get my self back. My self back. I mean to me that's a failure in the relationship: it took my *self* away. But the odd thing is that through it I became more myself than I ever was.

I guess I don't understand it all yet.

NEIL

I MET Philip in a writing class at the New School. He had long golden hair and one of those eternal-looking suntans that never goes away. I had just ended a very dreadful month-long affair with somebody and I wasn't looking for a relationship. I'd been in Europe for six months and just gotten back and took a writing course to get in touch with my writing again and I saw Philip sitting four rows in front of me. Quite honestly I didn't think he was gay. I kept saying to myself, "even if he's not straight, he's real young, Neil." Because he was twenty-one at the time and I was what, twenty-four?

1

And I started talking to him and a couple of weeks later I asked him to have coffee at this raunchy coffee shop down on Christopher Street. We talked and talked and I asked him if he was gay finally, and he said he was bisexual or something. He was involved with this very beautiful woman. I was obsessed with him. He had a really classical face. I'm usually turned on to people with something slightly wrong with their faces. Not drastically, but just something that I find very primitive, almost. And he wasn't primitive, he was anything but.

So I started trying to date him and he came over one night and I pounced on him. And he was really stand-offish. I thought he was real cool, by the way, a real cool guy, laid back, Southern like. He wasn't being direct. He was being evasive about all his answers. Which was a nice change for me because

I'm usually involved with very frenetic people, and I'm usually only attracted to very intense people, but in this case it seemed different. He was Jewish, but he wasn't New York Jewish.

Anyway, we tried to fuck, but I was tight and somehow it just wasn't working. I don't know why. All right, that's life. You know, you win a few, lose a few. And he left. I was very depressed, and what does a depressed writer do? He writes a short story about what just happened. Ironically, two weeks later both Philip and I were picked to read our pieces in class. Philip had written a piece about his ex-girlfriend or something and I had written a piece about Philip, which was very graphic and which freaked the whole class out.

What was the impact on Philip of hearing the story?

I think he was mesmerized. I don't know at this point what his real reaction was. His piece didn't work, the teacher told

him; and mine did, very obviously. Knowing him as I do now, I think he might have felt a lot of competition. On the other hand, I felt it was only right since I was older. I'd written a novel already, so it wasn't as if I was a total novice at writing.

In the second photo, Philip had just gotten out of school. I think he had to get a job, so he had all his hair cut off and that's what he looked like. He dragged me to all these barber shops, and I pay three dollars for haircuts. I don't approve of spending fifteen or twenty dollars. That's when I started getting very suspicious of Philip. I was falling in love with him, but as I was falling in love with him, I was seeing all these things I didn't like. He had an almost lethal attraction to sophistication, and he holds me responsible for that because in the beginning I kept telling him he had all this ratty clothing. I told him if you're into sex in life, you should dress like you're into sex, and he did a turnabout. Then he got this haircut and it was a disaster. He looked like an Upper East Side faggot. I made no bones about it. At the same time I didn't care.

You told him that you hated the haircut?

No. But I didn't care. I was falling in love with him. I made it clear it wasn't the kind of haircut I approved of. But at the same time I told him that it really didn't matter. That he was so beautiful he could get away with it. He's one of those people that gets away with anything. He really gets away with it.

But the big climax of that whole time was when his friends, Terry and Sally, gave a party. They were very key people in his life, sort of the nice mother and father figure. I think Philip was in love with Terry. Not surprisingly, I looked something like Terry; I had the same Jewish motherly attitude as Terry. Those pieces fell in later after I met Terry. Anyway, they were having this party for Sally's birthday, and it was the first time I was invited to meet his friends, his family. This girl Sharon was also invited and unbeknownst to me she had dropped three Valium to deal with the situation. I didn't drop anything. I wasn't taking any drugs then.

And so I go to this party out in Brooklyn. A real incestuous, lovely kind of setup. Everybody's real close and real warm to each other. My family is real close, but I don't have too many friends. I just don't. Now that I do the radio show I know a whole lot of people but I don't have many friends, you see. And it's a real lonely life for me. But that's life. So I really liked the idea of getting into this family. And then Sharon walked in and Sharon was dazzling. She was the most beautiful woman I've ever seen in my life. She had a pristine face, perfect hair, this long, long—I don't know, what was it, gold or brown or something beautiful—and she had these dazzling eyes, a svelte figure, and she and Philip were a perfect couple. And I was beginning to feel real guilty. I was destroying this perfect couple. I was doing my darndest to destroy this perfect couple. I saw them dance together and they were a vision out of *Tristan* or something, they were just so beautiful together. But in the meanwhile Sharon was freaking out of her mind.

Were you having sex with Philip at this time?

Yes. But it wasn't all that good. [*laughter*] We had this big dispute because I hated going out to Brooklyn. He was living near Pratt. And I had this big apartment and this was my fortress, and I was older. He lived in a pseudo-beat apartment, which means a very expensive, sort of Upper-West-Side type of apartment in a brownstone or in a wood frame house or something. I don't remember it too well. I just remember it was too modern for me and had too many conveniences and I was beginning to distrust him for that.

But I was falling in love and I had to figure out a way to get rid of Sharon. I wasn't about to share him, and by the time of the party he felt pulled equally in both ways. But I felt I had lost. I was feeling devastated at the party because I felt she had won. She was far more beautiful than I could ever conceive of being and he had been involved with her for over a year, so she had an edge on me. Plus Sally and Terry, everybody there, was making it clear who they favored.

I was getting real freaked out. So I finally dragged Philip into the bathroom and said, "Look, I give up. I'm leaving." Philip didn't want me to leave but he was totally freaked out too, out of his mind. So I left and walked to the subway and I kept turning around, hoping he'd follow. It was sad, but that's life. I get home. I go to sleep. Two in the morning I hear this knocking at the door. I wake up and answer the door. It was Philip. He didn't leave until two and a half years later, basically.

About a month and a half after that he came and—bang zoom—railroaded me into letting him move in. And I had real doubts about him. He was still cool, but he was getting very pressury. I was getting a little nervous. He had to really convince me that it was the wise thing. I thought it was the craziest thing I could do. I was against it, but I did it. He moved in and I got physically ill. Physically ill. I was on my back, I couldn't move for four days. I felt like I was on my death bed. All my friends would come over and sit on the floor next to me and console me. [*laughter*] I was freaked out of my mind. I was attracted to him because he was everything I wasn't. He wasn't earthy. He was sophisticated. He was just everything I wasn't.

Philip purported to be a real liberated person. I'm real tolerant. I'm like my father. My father certainly doesn't approve of homosexuality. But he'll go with the wind. If the wind is sort of pushing you to accept your gay son, you accept your son. I mean, I'm his son, right? And I'm real tolerant of what other people do because I know it's really none of my business, basically. And as long as I have a sense that they're really with me they can do what the fuck they please and I don't care. And Philip seemed to come off the same way. That was cool because I'm real promiscuous. And I was not about to have that curtailed because of love. And also there was another basic problem, and I think it was the most serious problem we had. I didn't have a primal attraction to Philip. I mean I was in love with Philip but Philip was not my ideal Italian. He was not even Greek. A lot of him was so familial it was frightening.

So what?

Familial. I knew a lot about him before even—we didn't have to say anything to each other. We had the identical upbringing.

We both had a mother who's a hitter; he had a laid-back father, I had a laid-back father; we had an older brother and sister who were extremely talented and bright. He had that liberal Jewish upbringing which I had—the only difference is everything was expected of him and nothing was expected of me. But other than that, there were just so many familial things which I think bring people very close but are very antiromantic. I think I need distance. A certain kind of exotic distance. And as long as Philip was a Southerner, that was real exotic to me. I could cream just listening to a Southern drawl. But once he moved in he became Philip. You know, "Fuck all the other shit. Fuck everything I'm presenting to you, now I'm going to be me." And what "me" was, was all of a sudden he got freaked out about everything I did.

I mean it was like a hurricane moved in. A little summer storm that turned into a hurricane. And I think the trauma of him moving in caused me to trick out a lot and I started watching television a lot. Obviously trying to avoid something.

So Philip moves all his shit in and gets this job at a photography store. Something ludicrous like that. It's a real wipe-out, boring job. So he would come home and expect me to entertain him. I mean you work at a boring job for eight hours, you come home to your lover, your lover is supposed to sing and dance for you. Do something. But I was working six hours on something I really loved, which was my novel. So I just wanted to relax. I didn't want to deal with this shit. And here, Philip turned out to be a heavyweight. You know, he wanted to analyze problems. I'm considered someone who's into analyzing problems in life and I believe it's real important, but he turned it into an art form—like analyzing the problem took ten times as long as the problem itself would take you. Nevertheless we weathered it.

I'm real stoic in life, and I believe that as long as the good balances out the bad I'm willing to deal with all the shit. I also knew I was rigid. A stranger wouldn't dream of calling me that but I knew internally I was and that I wasn't very loose with my feelings. I wasn't brought up in a family that was loose with its feelings. We're not physical at all. I'm the only physical one in the family. My father wouldn't dream of kissing me and my mother would kiss me on the cheek. Her mother before her was half German-Jewish stock and if you know anything about German-Jews, forget feelings. They can't relate to each other.

I don't think the sex went too well from the start. I don't remember. I don't think I want to remember. Sex was real difficult. I had never, for any extended period of time, fucked with one person four or five times a week. I was going to say one or two but it was four or five times a week, and it was a major achievement for me. It's interesting, 'cause until he moved in he could have fucked me anytime he wanted. Once he moved in he couldn't, and a lot of it had to do with my feeling very pressured by him after he had moved in. We would have sex, and he gets more into sex—he gets more into almost anything—than anybody I've ever met. I'll never forget this as long as I live: I would try to listen to music with him, since a big part of my life is music. I mean I was raised on it and I've been writing music for about thirteen years. And I cannot play Mahler to this day—I get too upset because of Philip. Because Philip would lie here on the couch and we'd try to listen to music together—I figured we could do that together—but he would listen to Mahler and he was in a world of his own. If you ever go to a discotheque and see all these cute fellows dancing and they're not dancing with their partners, they're dancing with themselves, it was like that.

Did your parents know that you were gay when you met Philip?

Oh yeah. Yeah. My being gay has been a very long journey— through being fairly actively bisexual, being exclusively gay, going back to being bisexual, to being exclusively gay. My parents found out in a very negative way—somebody wrote them a letter. Not for money or anything, but just to get back at me, and I don't even know who wrote the letter. This was back when I was seventeen—not too many people were *gay* then— and they were absolutely horrified. My father threatened to

write me out of the family and the will; he had never mentioned these subjects to me before in my life, so being threatened with being written out was very, very heavy for me. And I
had just won a scholarship to study in England, and England
had just legalized homosexuality. So my father was having con-
niptions! [*laughs*]

We went through this titanic struggle—I went to a shrink,
they went to the same shrink the next week, and the three of us
went the third week. It was the most frightening experience I
ever had, because the analyst accused my father of various
things just to get him to react emotionally. He called my father
a shit and all these things. I would say, "You can't call my
father a shit"—and my mother breaks into tears: "You can't call
my husband a shit."

What year was this?

This was '67. It got real heavy toward the end . . . my parents
were willing to put me up in an apartment in Manhattan as
long as I was going to go straight, and the analyst says it takes
at least five or six years to go straight, and I didn't even *want* to
go straight. So I said I'd rather not do this analysis and I'd
rather go to England. So my father pretty much gave up and
said, "All right, go to England—I don't want to deal with this."

And I left for England, and gay life in England, I mean, it's
hard enough here, but it was *really* bad there. So on my own I
decided, for strictly social reasons, that I wanted to be straight
—or at least very actively bisexual—and in fact my shrink
turned me into a very active bisexual.

How about Philip and your parents?

Philip and my parents. All right. [*pause*] He became one of
the family. Once I was very clear to myself about being gay, I
made it very clear to my parents—you treat me, you treat
whom I'm involved with, and I want you to take it seriously. If
you won't take it seriously, forget seeing me. And you don't
argue with this. I was very adamant about that. It was real
interesting to me, how the different people in my family reacted

to my being openly gay, because empathy came from very surprising places. My mother's sister, who is a very patrician woman, very refined, was wonderful to me. She was the last person I ever expected to be open about treating Philip as my spouse. I remember the first seder when he was living with me. She always had a seder. And she went out of her way to tell me she hoped that Philip was coming. And this was the first situation when a member of the family, other than my mother and father, knew that Philip was gay. I was really overwhelmed. I appreciated that so much. It was real important to me. Since this was my favorite aunt anyway, she really became a goddess to me. My mother finally admitted that she thought I was crazy. Which was her way of saying she finally saw me as an individual.

She was, she still is, real fond of Philip. She became a mother to Philip, really, because his parents live in Florida. And she and Philip would have these *heavy, heavy* discussions about sex—about everything. It was real crazy because my parents, every other Sunday or so, would take us out to Chinatown, and Phil and my mother would be in the corner talking about sex or something. My father would be going bananas: "Look at this painting"—and there are some hideous paintings in Chinese restaurants, right?—and he would tell me how beautiful they were. [*laughter*] Nevertheless my father is my father. He treated Philip like a son really; he was real nice to him and would ask him about my health—things that in-laws ask the kids.

Once my father asked me about my earring. He said at dinner, "Neil, does an earring in your left ear mean you're gay?" And my mother said, "No, of course it doesn't. It means that he's gay and he has a lover. And in the right ear, it means you don't have a lover." And I'm just sitting there saying, "Huh. Where did you read that, in *Time* magazine or someplace crazy like that?"

Philip and my parents got along real well.

What about Philip's parents?

[*laughs*] Well, all right. Philip came out to his parents once he was with me. I think usually gays find it's easier to come out when you have a lover. I mean, I wouldn't even recommend coming out if you're alone. When Philip moved in with me he had the strength to come out, really. I was pleased because I was very politically conscious and I was very openly gay, at least relative to a lot of other people.

How did his parents react?

Well, his mother, who is a very, very intelligent, liberal woman, began sounding like a Baptist minister in her letters. It was shocking to me. Really *unbelievable*, the kind of diatribe she'd write. She called our apartment *a den of iniquity*, and she called my mother *a fag hag* [*laughs*] . . . really insane things. It's that liberals just don't know how to deal with homosexuality. It just is not in their reality. At all. Since most people have problems about their own sexuality, it's no wonder there's so much homophobia. But with his mother in particular, I was the enemy. It was so obvious to me what was going on: it was a battle between me and his mother, and at the same time I wanted so badly that she would accept it. That she would accept me.

Did you ever meet her?

No. But I'll tell you a funny story. In a way I did. She was coming up to New York—his parents would come up periodically; she's a name photographer. The Edward Weston show was opening up at MOMA. I had to see this woman. The thing with Philip and his mother was that anytime he had problems with his mother he'd take it out on me. So he'd get a letter from his mother or a phone call from his mother and I *knew* that the next forty-eight hours would be hell. It was like being at the Marne keeping the Germans off or being in Leningrad keeping the Germans off [*pause*] it's always Germans, isn't it? [*laughs*]. This is how I saw his mother. Every time he would get something from her, he would take it out on me. At first he wouldn't acknowledge what he was doing—he was in a bad mood, he wouldn't cook, he wouldn't do this, he wouldn't do that, and it went on and on. I had all these fantasies of calling his mother and saying, LOOK, . . . WHERE . . . THE . . . HELL . . . DO . . . YOU GET . . . OFF, treating him like this and treating me like this. You know, she had threatened to come up and take him out of the apartment—it sounded like one of those deprogramming kinds of situations.

Anyway, she came up with his father to New York to see the Edward Weston show, so I was going to go with Susan— our friend Susan. I was going to pretend I was somebody else. But she'd never seen a picture of me either, so I didn't have to do that. I stood next to her through the entire exhibit. I stood right next to her; wherever she went, I went. I listened to her speak. And I'd watch her move. I'd watch her every single motion. I knew her backwards and forwards already, but I had to correlate it with the image. I was *so* dying to say something, to make some strange cracks to her—not as if I was me, just as somebody at the exhibit. That was no go. I really was not interested in his father. His father was like my father, real nice and real sort of laid back. At the end, his father was just about to deal with us, to meet me, at a meal or something, when Philip and I had a final falling out. I wanted to be accepted by his parents. I really did. I met his sister, we got along like *that*. We both had a very similar orientation, been through the sixties together. I understood a lot about Philip through his sister. Also through his mother—through his mother's letters and things like that.

But at the same time, I felt a lot better about my parents in contrast to his parents.

Do you remember when you fell in love?

Oh I fell in love with him the minute I saw him. I just melted. I mean I just melted away. He was so beautiful. He really was. He is. He had that eternal look and he had these real sad eyes. And he was really alive. I mean, so many men seem dead already and they were younger than I was. They're functionally dead. You know, they deaden themselves. They take on lovers and they go through the form of having a lover. Or they go through the form of going to a bar and picking somebody up. Or they go through the form of going to a discotheque. You know, they're all dead inside basically. Phil was alive. He was really alive. But he was dangerous. Oh is he dangerous. I'll never forget—I called my friend Paul—and Paul said to me, "You know, Neil, Philip is really beautiful. There is no question about that and he's really interesting and he's really bright and blah blah blah, and, Neil, he might be a little too young." That was the one thing that freaked me out—I'm not into anybody older or anything like that, but I am hung up on somebody who's too young. I always was. I like peers basically, because I think peers are emotionally in tune with you. But Philip was young and I knew it. I even knew at the beginning it was going to end. I knew he was going to leave me. I knew this and I kept blocking it. I even said it to him at the start: Philip, I know you're going to leave me. And of course with that kind of atti-tude, it's little wonder it was set up so he'd leave me. So I'm just as responsible as he.

And when he left?

I wasn't shocked. No, by the time he moved out, so many numbers had been pulled and I was fed up with him and I gave him an ultimatum basically that he either put up or leave. I didn't say leave. I said either put up or I'm getting involved with somebody else. And I proceeded to get involved with somebody else, but that comes years later.

The next one is the early photo of you?

Oh yeah, that one [3]. I would fall in love with a guy like that. I mean attitude. That's an attitude photo.

An attitude photo? Hard at work, serious young writer?

[*Laughter*] Exactly. Exactly the image I wanted, and that's exactly what he got out of it. That's exactly what he saw. I was a hold-over from the early sixties, not even the late sixties. I was too late for the late sixties, you know, that whole hippy-dippy trip. In the early sixties, that's where my consciousness was formed. The whole civil-rights movement, and the whole Dylan thing—that left the strongest impression on me. And in Europe for four years going to school, so I also picked up this certain kind of worldliness. I was real worldly.

3

Where did you go to school?

England. In England I spoke much better than I do now, real transatlantic English, so they couldn't tell whether I was a multimillionaire from Boston or a middle-class Jewish boy from Forest Hills.

What do you think attracted Philip to you?

I'll tell you what he claims to me, that it was my vulnerability. He also claims that I was only vulnerable for a few seconds. I mean the way he talks about me, anybody would fall in love with me. Really. For a few seconds a day I would be vulnerable and he would fall in love. I don't buy it at all.

Why do you think he did?

What?

Fall in love.

I don't know. All the things I thought were interesting about me Philip didn't think were interesting about me; and all the things I didn't think were interesting about me, Philip fell in love with, so that you know there's no accounting for taste in this world. Or for love. I guess I was sexy. I came on real strong with him. I worshipped him.

You were sexy but you just said sex wasn't so good for the first few months.

I was in love with him, I didn't care. In love you don't care.

But I'm interested in what you think in reality made him fall in love with you.

There was no reality, there was fantasy. Fantasy. There was no reality. I mean reality, there's a thin line between what the reality is of how Philip saw me and what the fantasy was.

Yes, but what was motivating him? Do you think it was sex?

No. I was real open in life compared to most people he probably knew . . .

You adored him.

I adored him.

Do you think it was that?

I adored him, I was very straight with him, I told him I was in love with him and he wasn't used to people being that straight. I remember sitting in a restaurant, oh God, it was over on Macdougal Street, and what did I say to him? I told him I wanted him. You know, I'm real blunt. I just told him I was in love with him and I wanted him. And he couldn't respond, didn't know how to respond. He wasn't in love with me at first. It was very obvious to me. But I also knew that I had my ways, and I would make him fall in love with me. And I did. And I just was myself, that's all I had to be, 'cause I knew that I was a real attractive property, right? I'll put it that way. I had all the outside qualifications . . .

Good-looking.

Yeah, I'm pretty good-looking, I'm very good-looking—oh God, that's a terrible thing to say on tape. All right, I'm good-looking, just leave it good-looking. I have style. I don't think I'm ordinary. I'm not your run-of-the-mill faggot, I guess. I have solid credentials in terms of involvement, you know, like political involvement. Solid Left credentials. Philip's sister has solid Left credentials, he was brought up that way too. So we had a very common world view. And I also had this European view. 'Cause I had traveled in Russia, I had traveled in India, I had traveled all over. I was obsessed with travel. We Sagittarians all are.

You think that was important for why he fell in love with you?

He was overwhelmed with it. I would be too, you know? Like when I meet a concert violinist, oh, I'm in love with him immediately, just like that. I think people get overwhelmed with credentials. I went to the London School of Economics, I spoke French fluently, I was nice. Not now, but I *was* nice. I don't know why he fell in love with me. I'm giving you all the reasons why he might have.

I was just curious what you think. You'll be curious when you read what he thinks.

I don't believe that. You see, I don't believe he's honest that way. I don't think he likes to ascribe superficial motives to himself. There have to be these real profound motives, and I don't think human beings are made up that way. I think we're made up of profound and very superficial motives in everything we do. I think I'm a very secure person to be involved with. I think he knew that. I'm real solid. I'm not flighty. Again I'm falling apart now, but I'm not generally flighty.

Photograph [4].

Me in the steam. I think Genet was the first person who opened my eyes to the night side, the life that goes on between midnight and dawn. And part of me is obsessed with the Satanic. Like S&M, I'm not into S&M particularly, but I was curious. But I never did it with Philip; I had him on a pedestal. And so whatever might happen in my "fantasy life," with Philip it was all romance. It was like a nineteenth-century full-blooded romance. He was right out of Botticelli. That's the only fantasy I had with him really. Botticelli.

This photo is the side of me which Philip felt real ambivalent about. This is the demonic image. The look, the attitude, the demonic attitude, which I can pull off real well. It's like sweat. Have you ever met people who say they don't like sweat? Well if somebody ever said that to me, I'd throw them out of bed on the spot, not because I'm obsessed with sweat, but anybody

who'd actually delineate the fact that they don't like sweat belongs out in Scarsdale, sleeping in separate bedrooms, really.

I've always seen myself on the fringe, and I've always related to the fringe writers like Rimbaud, and I told Philip to take that picture, 'cause that's how I saw myself really.

Moving right along . . . did you have more to say?

Oh I could talk for hours about myself.

5

Number [5]—Philip as St. Sebastian.

No. It's not Philip as St. Sebastian. That's not St. Sebastian! It's Botticelli! The Botticelli David. [*very long pause*]

OK. Would you rather talk about [6]?

It shows all my ambivalence and all my anger and all my hurt rolled into one. And it just so happens that I had just got out of the hospital. I was run over on Canal Street and knocked up in the air and down on my head and I had twenty stitches in my head, and my leg was banged up. Now I expected a lot of sympathy when I got out of the hospital. I got to Provincetown and people were treating me as if it was just good old Neil. And here I was having three migraines a day, I was just not in good shape. And I expected to be treated with all due respect.

6

How did Philip treat you?

[*Pause*] Philip was petrified. There was a lot of love there, but I just felt that he was treating me like one of Laura's things in her Glass Menagerie. Like anytime I moved I was gonna break something. He was like almost crying every time I walked. He was always afraid I would knock my head against something. He would almost break into tears.

He was scared?

Yeah. He was real scared. And like he really took care of me, I have to say, he really took care of me. He really thought I was going to die.

What do you think this photo shows about you?

Oh, my sense of eternity. Just eternal longing for something, you know, I'm always longing for some sort of happiness. But to get it, God, the hell you have to go through for a little happiness. You know, it's like artichokes. Like all there is to the artichoke is the choke basically, and yet you have to go through all this, it's really heavy when you buy it, and then you suck off the leaves and get to the choke and there's barely anything at the choke. And it's like what you have to go through in life; for a little happiness you have to go through so much, so many hours and months of shit . . . I remember this guy I was living with in Paris for a while. Said I had the saddest eyes he ever saw in his life. Maybe that's what this photo shows: the saddest eyes I've ever seen in my life. Isn't that pathetic?

Look at [7].

That's Neil the iconoclast. 'Cause Neil's wearing a football shirt and a black leather sports jacket, and his cane ('cause my leg is messed up) and Terry's cowboy hat, and you know I never fit in.

How do you mean, never fit in?

Oh, being gay, being a writer, not having a nine-to-five job. In relation to my parents, it was a lot harder for me to be a

writer than to be gay. It's a lot harder for them to deal with my being a writer, especially a writer who has not sold his first hundred-thousand-dollar novel. You know, my mother listens to these radio shows all the time to get me advice—all these writers whose third-rate novels have sold twenty million copies telling how they actually did it. She wanted me to write about face-lifting! I said, "Look, you want to write about face-lifting, you write about face-lifting. I don't want to write about face-lifting, I don't write about those things." The situation got worse when I started writing exclusively gay stuff . . . I'm sorry I did, in a way, but I did and I'll have to pull out of it. But there was a point where I was doing music reviews for the *Voice*, I was doing film reviews for *Soho*—I wasn't doing gay stuff at all. And then I just got myself very, very involved with the gay stuff. And I started writing exclusively gay stuff and then I got the radio show. I was asked to do WBAI's gay show. My father and mother didn't want me to do it. The thing is, I had already promised the listeners that I was going to have my mother on my first show. My father wouldn't allow that. Still, they had to deal with the fact that their son was doing a gay radio show, their son was a gay media person.

How did you feel about the show? Did it take time away from your work?

The problems got very complex: I had a number of friends from my CR group who were successful writers and who warned me about getting trapped in gay media, becoming typed as a gay writer. But since I could see a wealth of things to write about in the gay world, I wasn't that concerned. I kept writing different record columns, even if they were for porn magazines. I was still listening to records and keeping in touch with criticism, which pays bills. I always had gigs from the time I met Philip, I always had regular monthly gigs to write. And given my rent—which when I met Phil was seventy-six dollars, which meant thirty-eight dollars apiece—it doesn't take too many of these gigs to stay afloat. And when I couldn't stay afloat, I would sell first editions or sell records or something. I just had a knowledge of all these crazy things, which I think free-lance people have to have in order to survive being a free-lancer.

How did your work affect your relationship?

Well, I made the terrible mistake of trying to write a novel contemporaneous to the facts, of trying to write a novel about my relationship with Philip.

Why did you do that?

It . . . it just flowed. When I met Philip, we each read our pieces in class. This guy went bananas over my piece. It was like such an ego trip that I just turned it into a novel. If he likes that, he's gonna looooove this! In fact, he loved parts and he hated parts. But I can't take criticism for shit. I don't think most creative people can . . . The relationship was so dramatic from the beginning, it was just so filled with drama—I don't know if it's just we were very dramatic people, the fact that we both loved drama. My mother always accuses me of that. Of loving drama. That's an accusation coming from my mother. The writer in me just saw all these possibilities. Plus I got ego food from my writing mentor, who sent me to an agent—agent number one. [*laugh*] I also wrote music. I was writing songs about the relationship.

How did Philip respond to the writing?

First of all, to get him to read it was a major chore. Because he'd try to find the lamest excuses not to have to read it. I need approval but I also need encouraging approval. Philip didn't wait to get the feel of anything I was writing, a general overall thing. He would start, you know, he would start, and he was really very critical and that's not what a writer needs until the final draft. And now I realize that. Now I won't show anything to anyone until I've reached the final draft on it. Because it destroyed me. Plus he didn't like some of my characterizations of him. And he would be upset. It got crazy. The novel got crazy. I'm still on the third draft, the third draft I did rough, because I didn't like it. I was bored with the whole thing. I was getting schizophrenic—which is the novel, which is the alleged relationship?—it would drive me bananas . . .

In general, Philip didn't respond in ways that gave you much support?

Well, whenever we had a major blowout, I would retreat. I didn't fight. Now I'm a fighter. I didn't fight then, at all. My weapon was retreat. I'd just get real silent and not say A WORD to him. That would freak him out completely, nothing worse than silence. That's the deadliest weapon you can use with anyone. Eventually he would say that he took it for granted that I was a quality writer, the kind of quality we both liked in writing . . . but in fact I *needed* that encouragement, desperately. I mean God . . . you know, creative people need so-o-o-o much ego food, it's unbelievable . . . when I think of the ego food I need, and some of the gigs I've taken just to see my name in print, because I was working on a long piece and it took a while and I wasn't getting ego food . . . so you write these stupid things . . . just to see your name in print in a different type size or something. [*laughter*] Philip didn't understand that . . . and Philip also had so many needs of his own— I mean, God, he was 21 when I met him . . .

How about Philip's job?

Okay, yeah I think he was working a straight gig, but I mean we both had the perspective on it so that I accepted it in him. I thought it was just a step for him, you know. He also had much more nine-to-five tendencies than I did . . . I've tried to get a lot of nine-to-five jobs, I really have. I've tried for some of the most ridiculous jobs . . . and there's this whole song and dance about being overqualified . . . and they are really afraid of people who have interesting credentials. They sort of want droney kinds of people in corporate jobs. But I *wanted* one corporate job so badly. I wanted to earn twenty thousand dollars a year. It's not like I lo-o-o-ove being poor—I don't think anybody poor just *loves* being poor. But if you have anything that makes you

individual . . . I don't even like being an individual. I've always
tried to look and act like everyone else. I have worked so hard
all my life trying to fit in. I have gone to the most OUTLANDISH
lengths just to fit in . . . and nevertheless I apparently don't.
Because I couldn't get any of these goddamned *Newsweek* jobs
—you know, the president's twerpy daughter can get these jobs
and me with my goddamned degrees and my writing experience, I cannot get a fucking job. You know . . . so I, so I
accepted the fact that I can't get a job, and I do my free-lance
gigs . . . but underneath it all I'm a very conservative person
who would like a house and would like a lover and would like
two dogs and two cars and all this shit, but I don't know if it's
in the cards . . . I really don't. And that scares me that I don't
even know if it's in the cards. You know, I, I, I get real depressed, like because—I don't want to become a businessman
and I'm very good at it—I'm very good at business . . . I'm
very good at buying things *real* cheap . . . I have an instinct for
antiques and all that crap—you know, and like I have this
DREAD—my great fear is that that's what I'm going to turn into
. . . that I'm going to become like all these other frustrated
people and turn to these professions not out of desire, but just
because I didn't make it . . . I remember in high school all the
drama teachers who were, like, failed actors and they were
always so goddamned dramatic. Whether they were straight
or gay, actors are actors, and failed actors are failed actors, and
I didn't want to be a failed writer, I guess, you know and
like . . . you try to reinforce yourself by going over all these
great writers who were never published in their lifetime, you
know, it's not a question of me not being published in my own
lifetime, it's a question of so much crap coming out . . . [*long
pause*]

How about Philip's work, his photography?

Oh, I pushed him to do it, I pushed him and pushed him and
pushed—I loved his work. I didn't like his garden scenes or
anything like that, because the only pictures I like are pictures
with people in them. Nothing works for me unless there are
human images in it. And of course the only ones Philip liked

were the ones with no human beings in them. [*laughter*] His
favorite photos are the ones he took in Paris when he went
there before he met me, of the Luxembourg Gardens or something like that, and I just found them boring. Then Philip
started taking pictures of me, because he was my lover—lovers
take pictures of each other. And I would take pictures of him
and I wanted him to teach me how to use the camera, and he
didn't really want to teach me how to use a camera . . . You
know, he wasn't a teacher. It's as simple as that. I would try to
go to museums and I wanted to learn from Philip because you
get tired of playing a certain role, you want to learn from the
person you're with, and Philip would get into a very pedantic
state of mind—and I would storm out of the museum . . . But
he taught me so much about emotional interaction—that sort of
balanced off things. I taught him about everyday realities, like
about shopping, and all these crazy things I knew how to do,
even about appearance. Now his appearance is much more
studied than mine is, but then it was the other way around. I . . .
I . . . always like to think I sculptured him, you know like I
created a Frankenstein. [*laughter*] I always see that. If it
wasn't for me he wouldn't be involved in this whole . . . uptown
mentality . . . he's not really involved in it, he sort of has a
perspective on it, but he's . . . [*pause*]

You respect his art?

Oh yeah, yeah, yeah . . . we used to fight about hanging
things up. I would hang some of his photos and he would rip
them down, I would put them up—I would frame a drawing
and make these mats. I would spend *hours* making these goddamned mats. I was a shitty mat-cutter anyway—but, you
know, I really loved his drawing. But he wouldn't even let me
—this is interesting—he wouldn't even let me *lo-o-o-ok* at his
photographs without him being there. He had to be sitting right
next to me, for me to look at his drawings or his photographs . . .
and I thought, yeah, I thought this was looney. It's like—why
can't I just look on my own? I mean that's really when you look,
is on your own. When you're looking with somebody, especially

with the artist there, it could make you a nervous wreck sitting there and you can almost hear him saying: What's he thinking? What's he thinking? You know . . . so . . . there was probably a lot of competition too.

How about [8] Neil the cruiser.

Yeah. Neil is a real hot cruiser. Neil does it with the best of them. Neil knows all the forms; Neil knows all the games. Neil's best on the street. Neil doesn't do too well in bars. But on the streets I am real hot, 'cause I just know how to do it, and I'm real quick and I'm real blunt, and I don't get turned down too often. That is like a big joke to me at this point.

My image had suddenly come into vogue, the image I've had now for what, ten years? I always refused to bend too much to what gay society was demanding of me. I had gone through that in '65, and I just didn't like it. Like wearing button-downs —it was ludicrous.

Now I did real well. You see that's not a sexy photo to me now, but I guess it was then. It wasn't even sexy then. I mean that's not sexy the way Philip was, that photo of Philip is sexy [9]. That's really Philip as a hustler.

Does that turn you on?

Yes. Well, yes and no, I mean, my hustler image in general is much more Italian, much more raunchy, much more mean.

That picture looks to me like he's trying to ape the type of sexuality that you're putting on.

He tried to do that every so often. I think he tried to do that because he thought I'd be attracted to it. 'Cause obviously if I was doing it, I'd be attracted to it. His attitude was, anything

you did, you were also attracted to. Anything you did in bed, you also wanted done to you. He believes that.

To go back for a minute, what was the context of [5]?

Ah . . . I had a friend named Frank from years ago. Now Frank was just a lovely Italian guy. I happen to think that all Italian guys are lovely on principle. But he was real down-home. He wasn't intellectual but he had real street smarts. I really dig that. And also we were opposites. We never had an affair, really, but we fucked a couple of times. And he was living with a guy in Connecticut, this guy I wasn't crazy about actually, from a farm or something. And Philip and I had one *ménage* with a friend and his lover. And I had the most wonderful time. The four of us were fucking; Philip had something like seven orgasms. Just about went out of his mind. Anyway, next morning we did this Monday-morning quarterbacking and Philip was freaked out of his mind. Absolutely. I couldn't believe this was the same guy who had such a night, who had so many goddamn orgasms. I can't have seven orgasms. I can have four maybe, but seven is a lot. And I said, "What's the matter, Philip?" He said "They were more turned on to you than to me." I didn't believe it for a minute. It turned out he was right in a way; it was a little marginal, I mean everybody was fucking around, and my God! It just pinpointed a problem in Philip. I mean, okay, you start off saying all men are competitive, but Philip goes above and beyond that, at least in this relationship. In the beginning he did. And I'm competitive to a degree, but only when I feel my situation is really in danger. That happened later on. But at this point, Philip was real competitive and I couldn't understand it, because he seemed to be having a good time—but he said he was real uptight. And this is somebody who was preaching all kinds of open relationships and being able to relate to people other than your lover and how it's valuable and how monogamy sucks, or not so much sucks, but it's not necessary. I don't take the position that, philosophically, promiscuity is necessary, it's just one of my own needs, 'cause I have never met anybody who satisfies me sexually completely.

Wait a minute. The first ménage was a real problem, because Philip was freaked out because he thought the guys were more attracted to you. Then you went up to Connecticut . . .

Then we went up to Connecticut, and I didn't like the owner of the place from the start. He was real cold and efficient. You know he was butch, butch. And, uh, we eventually fucked and it was a disaster. And I turn around and I see Philip getting fucked by this guy and this guy has an unusually large cock and when I saw Philip being fucked by somebody else, I just— "That's enough, we have to leave, Philip." I was absolutely freaked out. Absolutely. I couldn't believe I was freaked out. Just seeing Philip getting fucked blew my mind. Nobody fucks Philip but me, you know? Nobody does. I tried to be cool; I mean I'm the one who's arranged the whole thing. I couldn't get it off with Frank, I mean Frank and I were not relating, and I think this photo [5] was the next day. Philip and I went into the woods. We got undressed, it was real nice. And I'm not a woodsy type. But it was real nice. We just ran through the woods and we had sex and I asked Philip to pose the way I saw him, which is just like this, and that's the way I'll always see him.

Okay let's go on, do you want to discuss the picture [10] of you on the deck? The cat is going by, your feet are curled up.

Well I don't like cats. I don't remember the cat. I was really upset by that point. This was after we got back from the woods.

You were back together again, and you basically had overcome the problems from the night before?

Yeah, I think we had even agreed to leave earlier than we'd planned to, and that made me happy. I don't know why I was so miserable. I couldn't stand the guy we were with.

Because he told me that in the morning he'd woken up and he'd gone off to the other bedroom and had sex with this guy once again.

Oh that's right. I just forget these things. That's right, he did
do that. I was so miserable. You know, I was so unhappy. And
the only thing that made me happy was when we went to that
flea market that day; I was real happy at the flea market. I just
wanted to get out of there. We left that night. I was so miserable. I didn't want to see him touched by anyone. Didn't matter
to me if he did it and I wasn't there, but I was there and
watched this. And it also wasn't a *ménage* the way the four of
us had the earlier *ménage*, always interchanging partners. I
really felt the first time that communication was involved. The
second time no, even Philip would probably indicate there was
no communication involved. It was two people coupled off all
the time. I mean Philip has this problem; let me tell you about

10

Philip's problem. One of Philip's major problems is that he will
experience something and enjoy it, and then the next day decide that maybe he didn't really enjoy it. In his analysis I will
not even recognize what happened half the time. We will discuss his sexual experience of the night before. Like our sex was
not good. It wasn't bad but it was not good.

What was your sex? Who did what to whom?

In the beginning it was pretty loose until he moved in. And
then . . .

What do you mean pretty loose?

Well, we'd reverse position when fucking. And sometimes we weren't fucking. Sometimes we'd get off other ways. He will never acknowledge that that was a key thing, but it was.

What was a key thing?

His moving in and this whole Monday-morning quarterbacking just made me feel very self-conscious about having sex . . .

. . . The roots of my sexual problems with Philip go back to the kind of analysis I insisted on—my analyst helped me to relate to men only as sex objects, not emotional objects, not love objects. This was to get me in touch with women as both sex and love objects. It really was the kind of analysis . . .

Wait. Your shrink was saying it's all right to sleep with men as long as it's only for sex?

Right, exactly . . . But this is what I wanted. I figured that when I got straight, I'd be a happy bisexual. But the fact of the matter was after a couple of years I was unhappily bisexual. Although I always had heavy emotional relationships with women, I didn't really have good sexual relationships with women. They were just boring. I lusted after men; women were sexually boring to me at the time, so I stopped the analysis completely and came back to America. 'Cause I also stopped working. I had helped form a public-relations company in England, and after I formed it, I got bored 'cause public relations is really tedious, and I came back to this country. I mean, I was totally *screwed* up. I was totally screwed up because I was lusting after men but there was no way I could relate on any other level than sex, because I had trained myself not to see them as love objects. And I can't say heterosexual society was dumping on me, because I made all these decisions. Therefore, I wasn't bitter, really. I just knew I had to work this thing out. It took years and years and years—and I couldn't afford analysis, I didn't want to go back into analysis. I really had to train myself to see men as love objects, and take more and more chances with men sexually and otherwise. I wasn't particularly in touch with sex when I was twenty-one, twenty-two. I just didn't think about sex that much. I got off. I guess I would fuck guys; I certainly wouldn't get fucked. And I had oral sex—I wasn't really *into* oral sex the way one can get *into* oral sex.

I had a strange relationship with this American Indian guy— the loveliest guy I ever knew, the kindest, sweetest man I'll ever meet, who fell in love with me and I didn't fall in love with him. I just wanted somebody else to share things with, have a roommate. But he fell in love with me, and I warned him not to fall in love with me, but he fell in love with me. We lived together for six months in the same bed and did *not* have sex—I can't even imagine how he dealt with it. At one point he started to throw china at me. I was living on Hudson Street in the Village. I wrote a play and a musical just to escape from him. Eventually I found a place by myself on Crosby Street.

This was right before Philip?

The American Indian? Not right before. I went to India in between this guy and Philip. I went to Greece for six months in between this guy and Philip. And I was a waiter and I sold political buttons. I had these schizy little jobs.

This all resulted from my analysis—my analysis had worked, in fact. Yes, this is why love objects couldn't be sex objects. But I was working on it. You know, sort of getting closer to men and seeing them as love *and* sex objects, and being a little looser sexually but not really. And slowly but surely I saw this gradual progress, and much as I'm extremist in life, I was really pleased by this gradual process. I guess that's maturity, accepting gradual progress as opposed to these really extreme kind of Bette Davis situations. I got into an experimental relationship with two guys and it was very hard. I felt I was a central focus, that these two guys didn't like each other. I wanted us so badly to like each other and live together for a few weeks. Nothing more. This was a really bizarre relationship. This was sort of my experimental stage.

By the time I met Philip, I was real proud of myself. I had reached a level emotionally which I had never gotten to before.

I had come back a lot from my analysis. I had gotten back in touch with the fact that men were really my sex objects *and* my love objects. But at the same time I hadn't really had to deal with any kind of primal relationship. I hadn't had that in a while. I even had an affair with a woman at the same time I was living with the American Indian. To this day I don't know how men deal with it. I just put my feelings for women in the closet. I just don't think about it. It's hard enough to deal with men, and at least men I *know* I can get it up for. And so by the time I got to have sex with Philip, it was all well and good until he moved in.

What happened when he moved in, in terms of the sex? Before he moved in you were basically both taking the active and passive roles alternately.

Yeah, well he was taking the active role but he didn't like it, that was the ironic thing. I was forcing him to be active. Really. He was just out, he wasn't really gay. I don't think he's gay now. A lot of people say this to Philip and he doesn't quite understand or know how to deal with it, 'cause he sees himself as gay. I don't see him as gay; I never did, and never will. But he's Philip. That's the only way, he's Philip. Our sex got very routine. Sometimes it took a couple of hours and sometimes it took a couple of minutes. And he loved getting fucked; he loved it. And then one day he grew up and he decided he wanted to fuck as well, and to me it was just a process; I got him when he was in a process of growing. That's how I see it. A lot of guys when they come out feel they should get fucked. And in a way there was a whole Greek element I think. I was the older, wiser. Yes, he was very in touch with feelings and all that, but his wisdom in dealing with me was lacking. He would throw truth around, and had no regard for my feelings about it. He would be devastating in very negative ways. Believe it or not, I see the relationship as the most positive thing that's happened in my life. But there were some very heavy negative elements involved. He just went too far most of the time. He had me up against a wall, and you can't relate when you have one party up against a wall. He was always setting up definitions for how we were gonna talk about our problems.

I want to get back to sex. So you basically were the active person. Did you ever take the passive role?

I felt too threatened. I was afraid of him at first, he was stronger than I was.

In what way?

Physically. He could beat the shit out of me. He's real strong, physically strong. And I'm not. Now I am 'cause I've been working out. Then I wasn't. I had other attributes. I cooked. I'm a good cook. I cooked up a storm for him. I didn't cook for me. I didn't eat. I cooked for him. After a while you're standing there and you feel you're like Alice in *The Honeymooners*.

I don't think under normal conditions we would have related to each other. We would have seen each other as too powerful. But I think when you meet somebody in a classroom, or in a nonsexual setting, the relationship takes on very different contours than if you were in the baths or in a bar or something. It goes a very different route, I think a more healthy route. I think because I met him in a classroom, the whole thing was not so circumscribed by sex for me as it was for him. I think I was the first serious man in his life. He was the first serious man in my life. I'm basically a family man, there's no way around it. I want somebody to be there all the time. It's just too desolate to live alone.

Ever consider pets?

No. I've had two dogs. At one point I had two dogs, two rabbits, two finches, twelve old-world lizards—I mean you name it, I've had it.

To get back to sex.

My lizards are much more interesting than my sex life.

Who wanted more sex?

Oh he did. Jesus Christ. It's like it was never enough for him. You know we'd have sex five times a week, he wanted it fifty.

He claimed I wasn't in touch with anything. I probably wasn't.
But I never had a relationship with a man, so how the hell was
I supposed to know what I was supposed to be in touch with? I
accepted him . . .

Wait, wait, wait. You never had a relationship with a man?

Well, not so profound as with Philip. Philip and I had a very
desperate relationship. We were both really shooting for the
stars. And we reached the stars; but we also reached the pits.
Oh God, Neil, you're really getting tacky. Sex, let me think,
sex.

He wanted more sex than you did.

It wasn't just more, what he wanted was qualitatively
different.

How do you mean?

He said I wasn't tactile enough; he was very into touch. And
I always felt that he was too genitally oriented. Like he turned
everything into a genital situation as far as I was concerned. I
couldn't lie down with him without getting the sense that he
wanted to fuck. I was not all that in touch with my sexuality
when I met Philip. I guess I was considered hot sex for a night,
but anybody can be hot sex for a night. That doesn't take much.
It takes much more to have sex five or six times a week, which
later became two or three times a week, which later became
one time a week, which later became nothing. You know. I
agreed with Philip that our sex was too routine, but it was so
based on what was going on in the relationship.

In a purely sexual setting, there's no relationship to base anything on really, except the hour or two you talk to somebody.
But in the relationship that goes on, the rest of the relationship
ends up in bed with you. Everything that goes on in bed ends
up in the relationship. And from the time I met him to the time
he moved, Philip was working on a job that he hated. You
know, he was working at a photography store and then he was
working at Time-Life. Time Inc. goes against both our values

very heavily. Who takes *Time* seriously? And what idiots work for that magazine and push that crap on everybody? Philip, that's who! That's who does it, Philip! You know, I didn't taunt him about it because everybody's got to earn a living and in this society, if you're not working for a pig you're very lucky. Philip was very resentful because I didn't have to work regular hours. And I started getting published in the *Voice* sometimes. They were doing my music reviews. Until Clay Felker bought it. And then *Soho News* hired me as their film critic.

But not very well paid.

Well no, the *Voice* was paying like sixty-five dollars a review.

You think Philip felt resentment because you didn't leave to go to a nine-to-five job?

Oh he told me he did. We were very blunt about our resentments toward each other, and that was nice, but he wasn't too blunt about what he loved about me. That's the irony. Yeah, he was very resentful of the fact that I didn't work. Or that for instance, my aunt gave me a color TV because my black-and-white broke down. By hook or by crook I get what I want. I find jobs like reviewing, in which you get records for nothing—I'm obsessed with music and I'm obsessed with books. And I'm obsessed with people. So what do you need: you need records and books and people. And chicken's pretty cheap. So you learn how to cook. Philip's a little different. Philip's upwardly mobile and he's very into sophistication and very attracted to it.

After he moved out I saw some of the guys he was dating and I wasn't particularly impressed because they were just a bit too sophisticated. They didn't have the kind of values I adhere to, and they were very apolitical. I can see him dating a guy 'cause he had a nice car. But I'm impressed by certain credentials . . .

Discuss photo [11].

All right, here was the problem I was talking about before, and that's primal attraction. There are different theories on primal attraction. I believe that something makes you primally

attracted to certain kinds of people. And I happen to be obsessed with dark people—Italians, Greeks, people I consider
dark.

Philip, of course, is not dark.

Not at all. Although he could possibly pass for Italian. But it
would be a very northern Italian. And Philip's thighs I thought
were real sexy. Like they were hairy and they were big. And I
always dug thighs; I still do. But every time I looked at him he

11

had so much longing in his eyes and I felt he wanted much
more than I could possibly give him. I didn't feel up to giving
him everything, I just didn't have it in me. I didn't have the
strength. I thought he was a laid-back Southern boy but it
turned out he was a high-pressure New York Jew. Brilliant and
everything else, and talented and beautiful, but very high-
pressured. And so am I. Not so much. I'm probably more laid-
back. And a lot more sensitive to other people's feelings. He

was totally insensitive to my feelings. No, strike totally. Not true. He was pretty insensitive to my feelings.

Why did you take that picture? You took it the same day as the nude picture, right?

Yes.

In Connecticut.

I think harping on that thing is a mistake. That was not the crux of our relationship. Philip happens to believe that unless something traumatic happens in which you prove your love, in a certain way it's not real. Only when negative feedback happens in a relationship is the relationship valid. He so takes for granted all the positive things.

Philip thought you had enormous sexual power over him.

No, no, no, no, no. I didn't have enormous sexual power over him. He created that power in his head. And the big difference is I didn't experience the power. I only experienced the pressure. And the major bone of contention in our relationship was power, and I felt he had the sexual power because he was so able to respond to me sexually, twenty-four hours a day. I thought that was a great power he had, 'cause I was always intimidated by that.

But I got the impression that his demand for sex was . . .

Inordinate. There was a big power struggle in the relationship. My power was in the kitchen, in the culinary arts and shit like that.

And his power was where?

I don't know if he had any . . . Well his power was sexual; not in that I was obsessed with sex with him, but I was guilty about it. I was obsessed with my guilt about our sexual relationship. The fact that he couldn't understand how I could go out and trick when I wasn't giving him the sex he wanted. He could never understand that. Philip could not understand that he was not my totality of experience, that I had other needs, fantasy needs. And I didn't want to mix fantasy and reality with Philip. I was very clear on that. I knew exactly what I was doing. So it wasn't as if I was stupid about it. I just didn't want to mix fantasy and reality. I couldn't picture myself talking dirty to Philip. I mean it was just ludicrous, I couldn't. I couldn't really think of doing any kind of "scene" with him. The one time we got even close to it was when we did poppers or we did something, and I got into a heavy aggressive trip with him. But I was freaked out for three days. I could not function for three days. And to treat Philip like that was disgusting. You see I had Philip on a pedestal. And when you have people on a pedestal, you can't be too carnal with them.

Why'd you put Philip on a pedestal?

He was a god. Philip was a god, and he was physically, visually, a god. He also acted like a god, I mean I always felt inferior. Everything was real theoretical. Philip is a real theoretical person. And I was the exact opposite. I would always say, "Give me an example," and he never gave me one fucking example of anything! Occasionally he pulled that trick on me and said, "Give me an example," and I would give him six or seven examples of what I was talking about. And I don't trust theory. He had so many theories, and every time he changed his mind about what the theory of our relationship was, I was supposed to go along with it.

You said that the power trip was a very important part of your relationship, and I'm curious. Putting him on a pedestal is a power play in a certain way.

Well, he had me on a pedestal too, so to speak. We were both on a pedestal. Yet we were both real, real, real, real. We were exceptionally real with each other. Not one stone lay, to this day lies, unturned. All he can do with me, all I can do with him, is talk about the relationship. It's like two historians getting together, two experts.

Once I was working in the London School of Economics in

the British Foreign Office library and I met this guy studying "Somalia in January 1889," and all he could talk about was Somalia. And that's how I feel with Philip. All we can talk about is the three years of our relationship. We can't go anywhere. And he admits certain things about our relationship that I was pushing for three years, but why can't you admit it when it happens?

One of the reasons Philip refused to admit things was that he was younger, too; maybe that's why. For instance, he would always contest things simply because I had said them. And the only person who does that in my life is my mother. Really. It's amazing. Amazing. And I didn't know when I got involved; I didn't fall in love with my mother. 'Cause he was completely different then. That's what's so astonishing, just like a turnabout.

There were lots of power struggles going on in the relationship all the time. Everything we did, everything. I wanted him to start cooking and he would argue because he worked eight hours a day, but he wasn't giving me the money. He always used this argument he worked eight hours a day, as if I was getting half of his money to cook for him, you know, like a wife. I said, "Look if you give me half your money, I will gladly cook. You don't give me shit, you don't give me a cent." Finally one day I was broke. I was flat broke, And I said, "Philip, you're going to have to support me, you know." I was petrified because I've never been supported by anybody in my life. And Philip thought it was a wonderful idea, you know, real romantic. Okay, so what does he do? Every time I need thirty-five cents I had to go to him and ask him for the thirty-five cents. I was getting more and more freaked out.

Was that after you came back from France?

No . . . Yes. It was right after that. I was just broke. I had seen it coming, but I wasn't really ready for it. And so now I depended on Philip. Now he had the power. And boy, did he misue that power! You know, I said to him: "Well, why don't you leave me thirty bucks?" He didn't want to do it that way; he wanted to dole out dollar by dollar by dollar. So this went on for a month, then I just said forget it. I am not going to rely on you for money. And it really upset me, because he's really bad with money. I'm not bad with money, actually. I was real lavish with him. And I didn't care either. When I gave him a big birthday dinner, I spent three hundred dollars. I usually spend forty-six cents on my chicken but I really wanted to, and I spent about four days cooking. Four fucking days. I lived with Indians and Pakistanis and they taught me how to cook real Indian food, and so I cooked like ten different curries, really exotic. Advanced curry cooking. And like all of our friends were there, Philip was there, and it was really a wonderful thing, I thought. And I never quite got the feedback from Philip that I'd hoped I'd get. You know, he might have been a little overwhelmed by it. But it was very hard to get positive feedback.

What was his reaction to this big birthday party?

. . . I don't know. He liked it. He was freaked out by it. He was embarrassed. Everybody was paying attention to him. He was real embarrassed by it.

Philip doesn't like attention?

I don't know! He likes it until he gets it and then he doesn't like it. He was very freaked out by it. I don't think he understands what people see in him. And he never understood why I loved him.

Why did you love him?

I don't know why. Turn the tape off for a minute.

. . . . .

The question was why you loved Philip. [*pause*] **Do you want to talk any more about that dinner party?**

I throw the best dinner parties. Ask anybody. I really do. It's one big family. Everybody just stuffs themselves silly. There's a lot of dope and good conversation. That's all you need. And you don't need room either. Everybody has the idea that you need room for a dinner party. You just have to have a table and know how to cook and know interesting people. And anybody can know interesting people if they're interesting. Why did I love Philip? Philip was everything; he was my life. I wrote a book about him. Why do I love Philip? He was everything a human being should be. He's so pure and, really, he's so innocent. It's unbelievable. Why do I love Philip? Jesus. Can we do that question later? That's a really . . .

How about photo [12]?

That's why I love Philip.

Philip in the cap.

Philip was so arrogant and so sexy and when I would see Philip at a distance, like on a street, I didn't recognize him, really. I said, Who is that arrogant son of a bitch? Where does he come off walking like that? Then I realized it was Philip. I said, Jesus Christ! He really has this arrogant walk, which is not the Philip I know, really. I'm the only person who knows Philip, really. Nobody else knows him.

I think only children are arrogant. And if you meet somebody who's fifty and arrogant, he's just a child. And Philip was a child in our whole relationship, which was probably the problem.

He was so self-righteous. I always felt he was never asking me a question to get an answer. He was only asking a question so that I could say, "Well, what do *you* think, Philip?" and he would tell me the real answer. We would go through this process where he would ask me a question and I would give him what I felt was my answer and then he would go right around and tell me what he really thought I was saying. Nothing to do with what I was saying. And this happened all the time, day in and day out. I don't know. I was happier then. I was. It's like with all this shit I was so happy, I was so content. [*long pause*]

And we were very silly together; we had a whole language. I was *Baby* and he was *Duck*. He was *Weiner Duck*, he wasn't just *Duck*, he was *Weiner Duck*. And whenever we didn't want to deal with anything we just jumped into our baby talk.

Only when you didn't want to deal . . . ?

No, no, sometimes it was just a closeness. Like we were two kids together. In the beginning it was real nice, it was two kids playing with each other. But then we had discovered something that we could use when we just didn't want to deal with the reality of the relationship, all the shit that went down and everything. And so then we just started using baby talk just at every excuse under the sun. We really became obsessed with it. Now it's the only way we talk to each other. Not all the time, but it's as if we cannot be real with each other now with our feelings. I mean I've just come through six months of a totally fucked-up stomach. I'm sleeping alone. I'm miserable. Now is that justice? I ask you, is that justice?

You expect justice?

Yes! I always expect justice, I never get it. I am desolate here. He's in love. He's not only not desolate, *he's in love.* I'll never forget what he said when he called me up two months ago. He said, "Neil, I don't think I can ever fall in love again." I said: "Oh, really Philip. Really now. Give yourself a little time. In a couple of years maybe we'll both get over it and fall in love." Sure enough, last Friday, he broke the news to me . . . I owned him. I owned every inch of him. Every secret. It's the little things, not the big things, the little things, the little secrets you tell each other. It's waking up next to him, knowing his smell so well, incorporating him, thinking like him. That's what it was. See, he wanted everything, he wanted to mold me. That's what he wanted to do.

He wanted to mold you?

Yes, he wanted to mold me. I'm a rationalist, I guess. I see what somebody's about and I weigh things all the time—is the good outweighing the bad?—and if it is, fine. I'll accept the bad. But I accept the bad. He doesn't, you see. He really wants God. And he wanted to mold me into the kind of image he had of me. Just somebody who's like super-open and super in touch with all his feelings all the time. I mean part of his attraction to me was my distance. And he'll never accept that. He thinks it's all vulnerability, that's what attracted him—that's bullshit. I mean you know my physical image. That was always my physical image, like distance. I don't perpetrate it, it's just that I'm real uncomfortable with a crowd. Some people when they're uncomfortable do certain things. I keep a distance. I look real unhappy, or mean. Not usually mean, just real unhappy, and most people don't like that.

Did you have friends in common?

Oh, yeah. Well, I had a friendship of thirteen years, starting in seventh grade, and we both eventually came out and we were only gay together a couple of years, but we went through the sixties together. Philip hated this guy. By the time I had met Philip, I had also outgrown this guy. It started out, we were sort of surrogate lovers for ten years, we never had sex—we never discussed sex. We had a world of our own. We really did a whole trip together. And it was as close to a love affair as you can imagine, except there was no sex—there was a real bond, a real spiritual kinship. And Philip reacted violently to this guy. Everybody reacted violently to us together. The two of us had such a world of our own together over so many years, nobody could come near us. We were two kids in bliss; we had our own language. Phil hated him. It just so happened that I had seen myself really outdistancing this guy. When he came out, he went bananas, he went crazy gay. I didn't go crazy gay. It was real gradual for me. So I had outgrown him, and Phil was a good excuse to break away. And in that sense I was glad that Philip was so adamant about not being around him. Philip really could *not* deal with him.

And then Philip and I were both in the Gay Academic Union, and I'd been told later that we were viewed as the model couple. For some reason gay academics don't seem to have—or didn't then have—a very high sexual self-image. Sort of dowdy and dull, scholarly. Philip and I weren't like that at all. We were brash about our sexuality. We were intelligent, we were as intelligent as they were, certainly. We were real friendly; we had these dinner parties with them.

Also we had CR groups. Consciousness-raising groups which —everyone pooh-poohs them now—but they need it now more than ever. It's so obvious—all over the place. And Phil was in one; I was in the other. So Philip formed all these bonds in his CR group and he bitched like hell to them—and he created an image of me. They hated me. They kept asking him why he was still in this relationship. Like, I had some mortal enemies in his CR group who under no circumstances was I going to allow in the apartment, even though Philip liked them a lot. So he had a couple of friends whom I disliked intensely. Because I knew they were against the relationship. They were threatening me and I didn't like it. It was almost at the point where I was going to ask him to leave the CR group if it got too threatening. I watched his situation *very* carefully.

My CR group—we had an amazing CR group. It was like seven Jewish guys and one Italian who acted like a Jewish guy. In Phil's CR group you could only ask questions of clarification. My CR group, you could give opinions. There were weeks I wouldn't go in, I was so frightened to deal with some of those people. It got so heavy people would not show up at our CR group. It was a wonderful . . . it went on for two years. Everybody was on the raft of the *Medusa*. That's what it felt like, every week. It was an exciting, wonderful, important experience. And out of it, we moved in that circle—the politico-academic kind of circle.

And then there was Philip's—did I have any friends?—there was Philip's friend Susan from work, and I still have a very difficult time with her. She's the most insightful woman I've ever met and I have enormous respect for her. And I even have very powerful love feelings for her. She was hot for Philip when she met him. Of course, I was a rival. We acted like rivals whenever the three of us were in public together. And Susan and I still have this love-hate, this push-pull thing for each other. So that was always a volatile relationship. I didn't quite trust Susan, either. I saw Susan as a vulture. I really felt like a medieval knight. Protecting-my-fiefdom kind of thing: I have to protect what's mine. If there are any threats to me, I'm going to take care of the situation. I will tell Philip who we can and who we can't see. Depending on how threatening they are to me and how hostile they are to me.

Did you see a lot of friends? Did they constitute a society, a social context?

No, there were different societies. There was Philip's ex-professor Terry and his wife Sally and the kids, who were a big part of our lives. And they were a very good part, because they were a very conservative part, as a family usually is. They weren't conservative people, but families by definition, whether it's blood family or extended family, they're conservative. Philip had been infatuated with Terry, who was just a lovely, bright, sensitive guy. And I eventually realized I was a lot like Terry, a certain kind of machismo which is tempered with sensitivity. It's a sensitivity that people like Philip see bubbling underneath. Which they want to try and extract. You see, they need the machismo on top, to see the bubbling underneath. Philip sort of understands the contradiction, but doesn't quite accept it, the fact that you need one with the other. That's the only combination that Philip reacts well to. He's had involvements after me, but they haven't worked and I know why they don't work. 'Cause one of Philip's needs is to have that duality in the same person. It doesn't come that often, either.

With Terry and Sally I was paranoid from the start—Sally was not happy about the relationship. Slowly but surely I got to trust them more and more, and got to love them. There was Eddie, who was Terry's brother, and there were the kids. I get along real well with the kids. But I'm not crazy about them. I just get along with all of them, maybe because I'm one of them. [laughter] And it was family . . . and it was the best time of my life . . . from that point of view.

I understand why sometimes people get married or take on lovers for security reasons. You know, the sex isn't very good, and this isn't very good, and that isn't so good, but it has its security . . . and it's like, to be a single faggot in this city is a fate worse than death, it really is, and I don't envy anybody in that position. But to be part of a couple—and it's not a panacea or anything—it just reaches heights which make it all worth it. Also there are enormous amounts of time when you're just content. And there's no Virginia Woolf going on every day. Philip and I went through tons of times like that. Even though we had a very tumultuous relationship—you know, there were three and a half years of living together, so it's . . . like over a thousand days, and there were lots of long, just contented times when I didn't even think of whether . . . the question of whether Philip would stay or leave didn't enter my head. But Terry and Sally were real important in our lives. We compared relationships, and we . . . one thing you realize when you are tight with a straight couple is that there is *not* very much difference in the kind of problems that come up, and that you can— it's very easy to sort of interrelate the problems with each other.

Number [13] is Philip in the woods.

Oh, that was fabulous. That was the trip to France. This was Leonardo da Vinci's home. Philip was real in touch with nature. Whenever we went to the woods he was real happy and I

13

wasn't. I was miserable in the woods. I'm a New York boy, born and bred, and there's nothing that's gonna change that. I've had every chance in the world, I've been in the lushest valleys in India, I've been in those wonderful dells in Yorkshire, and I can't stand it. Can't stand it. Whenever I was in the woods with him, he was obviously blissful there. And I was jealous of his ability to be happy in the woods, because I hated it so terribly.

Why?

Oh I don't know, it was so corny. There were no films, there were no books, there were no records, there was nothing, no music. There were just woods.

How about [14]?

Oh, that's the Philip I love. He's almost elegant. He fits in. His whole aesthetic is so elegant. And mine obviously isn't. My aesthetic is comfort. Period. 'Cause I lived in a house where I wasn't allowed to sit in the living room. That is one of the Loire chateaus. It's the Gothic one. Not an elegant chateau. It was very heavy-handed; it's like Dürer. I'm obsessed with Dürer. I have a very oppressive aesthetic in terms of art, and I guess what turns me on is a very stark kind of art. This chateau turned me on. The more elegant ones, the Renaissance ones, I didn't like at all. And Philip just loved them. Just like that couch Philip has, which my mother couldn't believe when she saw it? That's Philip. And his throne. Have you seen his throne? The chair? Yeah. That's Philip. Even Mozart. I hate Mozart. He loved Mozart. Everybody I know loves Mozart. But Philip, somehow when Philip loves Mozart it seems so fucking elegant, you know, whereas Beethoven—or Wagner! When I was with Philip in France, I felt like I was making the royal entourage with Eleanor of Aquitaine. He was so popular. Men were just flocking to him every place we went.

How did that affect you?

On the one hand I wanted these French men to be attracted to me. Philip just happens to pick up these knock-outs who I'll

14

go after—and I do all right—but I somehow never felt I did as well as he did. He just picked up the most beautiful men I ever saw in my life. That's all. Consistently he picked them up. He didn't have to do anything, this is what killed me, he didn't have to do shit. I had to work my ass off to get these men, and he doesn't have to do shit. So he's had it too easy in life, that's my feeling. That's his mother's feeling. He'd hate to read that too. He's had it real easy in life.

Photo [15]. Philip being very angry.

Philip was being very scary. I always thought that Philip was going to try and kill me one day, because I could see it in his eyes whenever he got angry. I always felt he was holding it all back.

Holding it all back? I thought you said earlier he let it all loose.

Well there was a lot he didn't let loose. There was a lot more. I think at one time I saw murder in his eyes. I got back from

Portugal, and I was set to have a real relationship with him. I mean I was ready to give in on every single point, I was ready to get fucked and even try to enjoy it. I was ready to really give him everything he wanted.

This had become an important issue by now?

It became a predominant issue.

You getting fucked?

Yeah. It became a make-or-break issue for me. I was very conscious of the fact that if I didn't get fucked, the relationship was not gonna last. It was too much of an imbalance.

Okay, so then I came back, I was going to give in. Not that I hadn't given in on most points anyway. I bend, I bend a lot in a relationship. He doesn't bend at all, Philip. Really, he's not very yielding in a lot of ways. He's yielding sexually and that's it. He doesn't yield on anything else. And the way he yields sexually, he makes you pay for every grind you go through. I don't know what I'm saying.

Yes, you do.

He made me pay for every time I fucked him. He made me pay a heavy toll. By the end of the relationship I was a nervous wreck. I was as glad to get rid of him as he was to leave. There was no way out of that. We were both real sad. But it was such a relief. It really was. And we had been through a whole very obsessive summer of sexual release. And drugs. Lots. I mean I had never done drugs that way in my life. I can't say this: my mother's going to read it. I've got to stop this drug talk. All right: Philip. Philip was a bastard. I came back from Portugal and I was ready to give him everything. I let him know and strangely enough, as soon as I gave him everything he just didn't want it. I thought that was very funny. He made these demands. I was slowly moving his way in the relationship, opening up, being more loose and more open. But as soon as I gave him all, he just bombed out.

What do you mean bombed out?

He was not interested. He didn't want to relate to me anymore. The tables were turned. I had to pull everything out of him. All of a sudden I had to figure out what in God's name was going on in his head. And what was going on was that he wanted to move out.

Wait a minute. Where are we? After Paris, after France?

I can't remember where we are. I don't remember if this is after France or before France, it's a bit hazy at this point. It was some time within two and a half years of the relationship. And it was certainly after a year and a half. Anyway we were gonna split up and Phil was all ready to split up, and we were both really on the edge. And that night, what I did that night was, I mean I hadn't played Judy Garland for fifteen years. When I was twelve, I think I liked Judy Garland when I was twelve. I mean she has all the subtlety of a twelve-year-old. And I took out "Stormy Weather," and I played it and we both just broke into tears for hours, and we stayed together. That kept us together really. And we went to a counselor. A real good counselor. But the reason he was good was because basically he was saying everything I was saying in the relationship. That Philip was too possessive, that he was strangling me, and apparently I ought to strangle him. Or that Philip should just hang loose.

[16] and [17]. You and Philip in France on your honeymoon.

Not just France. It was Cannes which was the honeymoon. France was not the honeymoon for us. We had a car which we named Robespierre. And I couldn't drive stick. Even though I was gonna take this car and go to Portugal. I couldn't drive stick. Philip was doing all the driving, and that gave him a lot of power. He could decide when we were stopping and when we weren't. And he was supposed to teach me to drive. He taught me, gave me two lessons. And it got real rough. I'm a really good traveler alone, I've been doing it for years. But traveling with someone is something else.

We were camping out, we had this tent. We had just had the usual sex talk. I don't think we were any worse. Also I hadn't tricked out in all this time. I hadn't had any kind of release at all. And we went to Avignon, and we had a very good time at Avignon, there were fireworks, it was Bastille Day. Still the sex thing was driving us both nuts. It really was. We were getting hostile towards each other a lot, and I kept insisting we go on to somewhere else. We got to Lyons and I got intimidated by Lyons, it looked like a big city, I wanted to leave. And we went down the Riviera. Well, Provence is real beautiful, I love Provence, I always did. And the chateau country was really

paradise for us. And then we went through a real negative part, between the chateau country and Cannes. It was just dreadful. We went down to Arles, Avignon, and then we went down to Aix, which is just dreadful. Disgusting place. And we arrived in Cannes just completely unhappy. I never went to Cannes, because I just thought it was gonna be too expensive.

So we were ready to split, I'm ready to split, I'm always ready to split if I don't see what I want in five minutes. We arrived in Cannes and we're looking for a hotel and we finally find this place. And it was amazing, 'cause it was so idyllic. It was like a small Paris hotel with shutters, overlooking the street, a nice big bed and a douche and a shower and breakfast, all for like three dollars a person. Really cheap. And then we had the car. And the next day we went to the beach and we met some gay guys who told us about this incredible rock beach, a nude gay rock beach which is a little out of town.

And so we went there the next day and it was really idyllic, I mean all these beautiful naked men. And there was a woodsy part above the rock where everybody fucked and so Philip and I would go back there day in and day out and we started fucking and somehow because we were both fucking on the side and it was very open, and because we were real relaxed,

we were lying on the beach, and it's like we fell in love again in Cannes. Somehow. I don't know how, I can't explain the process. But everything was idyllic. Our sex life was idyllic, we were relaxed with each other, we could meet other people yet we felt this basic allegiance. And this went on for ten days I think, we just stayed and stayed. He was going back to work soon but nothing freaked either one of us out. He was meeting men. And one night we even met the same man. And it was just real nice, we really fell in love. It was like paradise. And I saw a lovely side of Philip, very unpressured. We didn't have these convoluted discussions, we just laid back. I'll never forget just sitting there in the morning, eating croissants, just looking at each other.

You were lucky. Do you want to talk about [16]?

Yes, the room. I had just got back from the beach, we'd been out at the beach and I was exhausted. And we always took naps. I've always taken naps, my whole life. But we always took naps. I figured we'd fuck later. That is me sleeping. And, yeah, I'm really happy when I'm asleep. I think. My sheets don't agree with me, they're all rumpled up when I wake up. Oh yeah, it was just paradise. We had everything.

And [17].

This is taken in the same room. Philip was very obsessed with mirrors, in our relationship. Philip would stand in front of a mirror forever. I can look in a mirror for maybe forty seconds and, like, everything's there. And I'm pretty secure about my looks; I know what I look like, and it doesn't change too much except for increasing lines, or the hint of lines. That runs in the family so I keep expecting it. But Philip was really obsessed with his looks. And it wasn't that he was vain; he was anything but. Insecure about it. And I would always ask him, "Philip, what in God's name are you looking for?" Even if we were just going to a movie or something he would spend an hour in front of the mirror trying to primp up or something. I couldn't figure out what he was trying to do. I used to get very angry at that, I

couldn't deal with that at all. I thought it was such self-indul-
gence for no good reason.

But did you think that he was vain or that he was insecure?

Insecure. Definitely. Oh yeah, we would talk about it . . .

Do you think Philip's looks have changed by the time of this picture?

Oh yes. When I met him, he went out of his way not to look
sexy. Went out of his way. He can thank me for looking beautiful now . . . Is that it?

**Not quite. I want to ask you what you think the differences
are between a straight couple and a gay couple?**

Uhhhh . . .

Do you think they're very significant?

Well, they are . . . they are . . . well penetration is the major
one. I think that there is just no real question with a straight
couple about penetration; the man physically penetrates the
woman with his cock. But I think with gay couples—we see the
cock as a very powerful force—it becomes a question of power
for me, of weighing things and deciding whether to give this
person the power to enter me, or whether this person *deserves*
the power to enter me. And it just—it stops becoming sex and
becomes something very symbolic as well. You know when I'm
getting fucked I intuit women, straight women. I really do, I
totally intuit them—I understand them so perfectly, which is
probably true of most gays and straight women, which is why
there is this incredible bond. And I have this relationship with
my mother, which I don't under*stand*—which I know is so tight
and so-o-o-o close and so Proustian almost . . . and the things I
intuit in her which I pick up in myself—it's scary. It's like part
of me is just like my father, very conservative, blah, blah, blah
. . . but the really major parts of me and the really subtle parts of
me, the emotional parts of me that are bubbling underneath the
surface, are all my mother. And I have this incredible connection

to my mother—it's not erotic in any sense, but it's like—it's unlike any—any emotional feeling I have for anybody else in the world. [*long pause*]

Do you think that's the only difference?

I think women are also more patient. This is just my general sense of women I've known. Women understand the importance of the primary relationship as a basis for society . . . really, their own positions in society . . . Women will put up with a lot more shit than men will. Especially gay men, who just run at the drop of a hat . . . whereas women . . .

Well, there's nothing holding them together.

Yeah, but even couples who don't want kids, I really see the women—and yeah, it's probably changing now . . . but I still think that women are a stabilizing force in relationships, and I don't see gay men as particularly patient. I mean *I* had a lot of patience. I could have run from that relationship so many times it just wasn't funny, but I really had to work—it was work—it was real work, you know, and I just had to do it, and I did it. But I enjoyed doing it.

What was the impact of the gay world?

On us?

Yes. I gather you didn't go out very often together, like to bars . . .

Oh we never . . . never, ever, ever, ever went to bars or baths . . . I wouldn't think of it.

So in terms of being together, the only aspect of the gay world you sort of entered was the politico-academic one?

Together, as a team, yeah. Philip did not like to be seen with me on Christopher Street—he's so competitive, so paranoid about who was looking at me. I figured most of the men were looking at Philip. I didn't care, I sort of prided myself in that— walking down the street with this really beautiful, sexy man.

You know, Philip walks in a room and everybody turns around
. . . Philip has a presence . . . he has a glow, and I don't think
many men have that kind of glow.

**Now comes the hard part. This is what, three years out of
your life? I don't want to ask you how you feel this week,
particularly. But if you can remove yourself a little from that,
what do you think about those three years, and this investment,
and this relationship?**

Well I grew up, and I became a man. Yeah, it's like everybody has their own theories about it; you know, Jews say it's
when you're thirteen.

And the Chinese say when you're thirty-five.

Okay, but I think it's when you love a man, only a man can
love a man. It was worth it to me. That's all I have. This
relationship. Was everything. It was my life. It was my life. It
was—I mean I loved him. Why would I want to deny three
years of our love?

Postscript / Philip Gefter

. . . he seems to value my mind and my various
talents more than this heart
of mine, of which I am so proud, for
it is the source of all things—all
strength, all bliss, all misery. The things
I know, every man can know, but,
oh, my heart is mine alone.

—GOETHE

WHEN I first read the transcript of my interview, I was horrified. It seemed that my experience of the three most profoundly felt years of my life was reduced to a chronicle of events devoid of the magic which made it so unique for Neil and me. The subtleties within our experiences were not conveyed by my words, yet it was in these subtleties that the relationship thrived.

To be sure, the relationship was more emotionally and intellectually comprehensive than is evident from the "sexual song" I sing throughout the interview. But, as passionate and emotional as was my experience of the relationship, I must acknowledge the emphasis I placed on the sexual dynamic. It was in the sexual arena that the needs I had and desires I felt for Neil were transformed into something tangible.

It's hard to summon a memory which truthfully contains my feelings throughout the relationship. I don't know if my retrospective view of those three years has been mythically tailored to accommodate my now self-protective needs. But when I read my own words about my life with Neil, I recalled many qualities of feelings I had throughout the relationship.

While I was living with Neil, I felt totally enslaved by my feelings. My needs of Neil were so potent that I had little control over them. I felt caught in a symbiotic web which I had woven for myself; any independent activity Neil engaged in made it impossible for me to function. I would experience exclusion, negation, and always felt that he was having a better time than I was. That soon translated into his life being more exciting than mine and, hence, richer. And, finally, if his life was richer, he was a more interesting and vital person than I was. Poor Neil; he suffered from my irrationally imposed conclusions, and I'm sure now that many of the dynamics he acted out in our relationship were prompted by my defensive, unyielding demands of him.

In retrospect, I begin to understand that the conflux of emotions summoned by any romantic involvement draws from that emotional network constructed in our initial, early-childhood attachments to our parents. The texture of my feelings for Neil

139

was similar to the most primary attachment feelings I am aware of. It's no accident that only Neil and my mother are capable of arousing primal rage in me, just as only they are capable of evoking in me those feelings of familiarity and warmth that I feel for no one else. It is at that level of emotion, established long before any of us are conscious of words to express it, where prototypal feelings and their construction exist; it is that same prototypal network which is reconstructed by romantic feelings.

Almost every couple I know experiences the phenomenon of baby talk. My feelings for Neil during our "sandbox dialogues" always reminded me of feelings I had when I was very young. I fantasized Neil as a three-year-old during those exchanges, and somehow, it seemed a way to strip all of his socialized behavior down to the vulnerable, innocent child which lives in us all. It was a way to try to connect at the roots. It was an attempt at the purest form of intimacy. (I often wonder if it was not also a manifestation of the genetic programming of the species to procreate—Neil became not only a surrogate parent but a surrogate child as well.) However, in the process of connecting with Neil on that most fundamental level, I lost my autonomy. Rather than growing mutually close and independently richer throughout our relationship, I only grew more dependent. When I finally decided I had to move out, it was as if I were reliving my weaning period from my mother. (My pet name for Neil was "Ween.")

Our relationship might have prevailed were the timing different. I met Neil when I was twenty-one, just out of college and in the world on my first real flight from the economic nest of my family. My sense of myself and my ability to survive on my own seemed awfully tenuous. It is no wonder to me now that I met Neil and fell in love after a month and a half of assessing and approving one by one his credentials against my internal checklist of ethics, background, intelligence, interests. It is no wonder that I became totally dependent on him. He was both more experienced and more autonomous than I was at that time. This is not to say that I wouldn't have fallen in love with Neil had I been older when I met him, but I would have approached the relationship from a healthier set of needs.

It was when I began to realize my strengths that the obsessive need to be attached to Neil abated. It was when I regained a sense of my own autonomy that I recognized the importance of my need to live alone. It became essential for me to discover my own independent, self-generating desires and goals. I think that any future relationship I have will stand a fair chance of surviving, because my needs will be different. I'll still have the fundamental needs for love, intimacy, respect, support. But they will be approached with a more established sense of where and how I fit into them.

A lot of very revealing testimony about our lives has been printed on these pages. It frightens me. It also becomes slightly absurd when I realize that it's "me" in the article I'm reading, and I'm reading about someone who's airing his proverbial dirty laundry in public. A little dirt never hurt anyone. We all know it exists, but few of us discuss it. I simply chose to discuss emotions and dynamics known by all of us but admitted by few.

Why have I chosen to reveal these most private of experiences? First, I honestly believe that those feelings which are private for me will remain private and even sacrosanct no matter how much I discuss them. I am still the only person who can experience my own life, and no admission, confession, description or explanation of my feelings will diminish my experience. Secondly, I believe that Neil and I are in pursuit of some unrealized existential truth about ourselves. To be able to see our words in print, removed from the experience of speaking about our lives, and to see photographs of ourselves juxtaposed against our account of their context, provided me a view of our relationship with added distance for observation. I expected to gain insights into our lives by being both subject and reader, and for me this process was invaluable. I observed both sides of my own words—the side from which I conceived and spoke them, and that side from which I read the words as if they were spoken by someone else. My words did not adequately communicate all that I assumed I was conveying as I spoke them, but paradoxically, they communicated a host of what became revelations to me about myself and the relationship. Neil's interview was revealing to me also; not because he said things I had never heard before, but because there was a distance imposed by reading them.

I was trained as a painter and a photographer. When I first moved in with Neil, I began to photographically document the relationship. Soon after I began the project, Neil demanded that anytime I photograph him, he also photograph me. That seemed fair, and even appropriate. One cannot, after all, document half of a relationship. I thought that by having photographs of us both, this chronicle would be authenticated. But as the project evolved, so did the obstacles. I can now look at these three years' worth of pictures, and recognize that I didn't grab for the camera at those *most* propitious moments—when we were embroiled in bitter dispute or luxuriating in utter and final bliss. I regret now that I did not have the presence of mind to photograph these moments of greatest meaning to me. The pictures which appear in this book are not necessarily the best images; they were selected because of responses evoked from Neil and me when we were looking at all the contact sheets.

Since I tend to be perennially ambivalent about everything, my reactions to these interviews are no exception. I'm embarrassed at how vulnerable I am. Yet, perhaps I'm just deluding myself in thinking that it takes a great deal of strength and lots of guts to go through with this project. I feel the need to explain, rationalize and justify so many facets of the material about Neil and myself, but I'll try to restrain that impulse within limits.

These interviews might be interpreted as self-indulgent, and I confess my own embarrassment when I first read them over. I wondered why anyone would want to read about our lives, about the tedious saga of two people who happened to love each other, about two lovers who hadn't the tenacity to make it work. Our story is by no means paradigmatic; it is simply the story of two men. Even what is idiosyncratic about our relationship may have its relevance in the lives of the reader of this book. I realize more and more that universals don't lie in generalized concepts of behavior; rather, they are manifest in the finite details in the lives of each of us. It is my hope that the dynamics and emotions we discussed will be recognizable to the reader in his or her life.

I believe that by publishing these interviews, we have offered our experience to provide a supportive base to those who feel that their problems are unique and, hence, doubly oppressive. I want to make it more comfortable for those who experience guilt or pain over what may be their own proclivities. Perhaps if people realize that they are not alone in the fundamental conflicts of their lives, the feeling of being a "villain," and the idea that their behavior is aberrant, will abate.

As for Neil, the other half of this story, we speak to each other almost daily. My feelings about him are primarily familial. He's the most entertaining person I know, and I still truly love him. We still do dances around each other and the games we still play are, at best, amusing, and at worst, adolescent; but the hysteria is gone. I no longer feel the need to connect so fundamentally with Neil. Intermittently, in more needy and excessive moods, both of us fantasize a future together in some form. I don't know if we will ever be able to live together again, but the need to resolve that question no longer presents itself with the urgency it once did.

We touched each other's lives. We loved each other and hurt each other. We laughed together; we argued often; we spent three years trying to get to know each other on that most fundamental level. It was the most valuable three years of my life.

Postscript/Neil Alan Marks

Oh beauty do you come
from the deep heavens, or do you
rise from the bottomless pit?
                    —BAUDELAIRE

THUS wrote a poet whose deep-seated ambivalence to women is well documented. In retrospect, I think my relationship with men in general and Philip in particular is colored by a similar love-hate hue. I have trouble painting my life with men but I can't create my cosmos without them.

I was initially surprised to learn of the go-ahead plan for publication of these interviews. It had initially been considered too esoteric a project for the hedonistic seventies, the decade when gay liberation was announced but never implemented. One of the reasons, of course, is that no one is sure what gay liberation means. Vis-a-vis the non-gay world, the questions appear to fall into two areas: legal and social. To many of us, the legal question is quite simple. As American citizens, are we protected by the Constitution or are we not? On a certain level, I sometimes think that the political/social position of homosexuals and lesbians in this country is analogous to the historical position of Jews in any number of countries. In terms of political rights for both groups, it is always a matter of now you see them, now you don't. This constant looking-over-the-shoulder affects the total fabric of our lives. We do not deserve to be devastated by the constant psychic and legal bombardments we must face from outside the subculture and within. Nevertheless, there is nothing to do now but build our lives anew. If more men, gay or straight who, like myself, are normally very private with their feelings would openly relate their experiences of other men on any and all levels, then less negative tension would occur in society. I am aware that many heterosexual men will be threatened by this book. One can historically understand the reticence of heterosexuals to learn anything from men who openly acknowledge their male love objects. Yet, I believe that anyone who has loved will be able to relate to Lovers . . .

At first, it was out of a sense of privacy that my initial surprise coagulated into stunned shock as I perused the typescripts of this three year journey. I read things which were at worst slanderous, and at best, in dreadfully poor taste. For someone like myself who relishes his privacy, publication of what is in essence a relational autobiography was an act of questionable

147

value. One question rang through my mind. *Who are you and why do you think your relationship is so important?* I thought that Philip and I were audacious in the extreme. Why then? The answer is difficult to come by.

I think I probably did *Lovers* because I am such an unlikely candidate. I am probably typical of a certain kind of man who experiences most profound joy and grief internally. So how did I make the leap from disclaiming the manuscript as slander to willfully posing for the cover? Perhaps it has something to do with being gay. I do not think men who get romantically entangled with each other have the same options as their heterosexual counterparts. The lack of legal ties probably has a more powerful psychological effect than any of us are willing to admit. I think if homosexuals want something to work, they have to work doubly hard. They can't say that they're staying together for the sake of the kids. They must work out day-to-day living arrangements. They must tend to what can be very uncomfortable interactions with relatives. If they are living in large metropolises, they must come to terms with the erotic lures which are not only free, but which know neither guilt nor respect for marital bonds. But little of this is written about. For all kinds of reasons, the gay press feels it is necessary to paint a rosy picture of gay life just as most non-gay publications feel the need to depict the opposite. The truth of course lies somewhere in between. But directness (or "truth") is something that everyone seems to find difficult. Particularly in the gay world, and specifically in the New York gay world, honesty is a difficult principle to maintain.

So, in a sense, you will understand my temptation to discuss the "Neil" character as separate from myself. It would be a way of not taking responsibility for the ambivalent characteristics I found in me. It is true that by the time I read the tale, I had emotionally grown away from the drama which, only two years previously, had been the marrow of my existence. I tried to read the manuscripts as any disinterested reader would. Lord knows I tried. But the "direct" part within me was fully cognizant that I was in fact being stripped naked of all defenses.

And in the gay world, defenses are the armor of survival. They have helped me run the channels of bars and discos. They have helped me slow my way into the port of a relationship and they have helped me steam my way out. This book could easily destroy my anonymity on the streets: my ability to maintain my chosen distance or to partake in spontaneous activity. And this is a serious loss. For the streets are a source of great energy. And whether the "street" is a tea dance in Pines Harbor on Fire Island or a softball game on Hayward Field in San Francisco, it is where the simple yet paradoxically complex gay social life takes place. And make no mistake about it. This subculture is as simple and complex as any other. And the fact that after the appearance of this book I might be looked at for reasons other than my physical presence made me feel quite ambivalent about the *Lovers* project. Don't get me wrong. I think there's a part in all of us which would like to get before the microphone and say *This is Mrs. Norman Maine*. But it wears thin. It wears very thin.

Perusing this manuscript I was able to perceive the ways I had and hadn't changed since Philip and I shared a universe during those turbulent years. Our relationship was the most profound nonblood tie I have made, and I only knew this after he moved out. I think that during the most revealing side trips on my Life Journey, I am not truly aware of their importance until after the fact. The difficulty is such: the highs and lows are so extreme that staying near the road of sanity becomes one's operative. I think that most people in non-traditional relationships wonder if they are sane simply because there is no literature to refer to. Philip was, in a sense, the Selma and Birmingham of my relational self. He was one-half of the struggle out of which was the promise of salvation.

And although immediate salvation was not forthcoming, ultimate happiness is in the cards. My reaction to the original manuscript of *Lovers* was a great test. My strong ambivalence about allowing publication boiled down to something totally unprincipled and mundane: vanity. I simply found the portrait of me unflattering. And who in his right mind would present an unflattering portrait of himself to the world? Thus, that part of me which is into packaging an appealing presentation elected to cancel the project. And I wonder whether it is because I am gay that part of me is into presentation. For homosexuals are, together with heterosexual women, sexual objects in the extreme. And what's more we know it and dress accordingly. That side of me which didn't think I'd "look good" in *Lovers* said "No deal" to the project. For weeks, I would alternately cancel the project and then reinstate it. Time and time again, I would get on the phone and indicate that this and that phrase, paragraph and even page must be excised. Finally, the battle ended decisively and I let the original manuscript stand as was, cutting only two or three sentences, at most, and one photo.

The reinforcements which turned the tide came from a side of me nursed from infancy by my parents, both of whom are highly honorable people. It is a side which never cared what the neighbors thought: a side which came to intellectual fruition during the mythic sixties and into an emotional blossoming during a relationship with one Philip Gefter. And it is a side which has been held in partial suspended animation in the gay world. It is a side which values ethics and honor and honesty. Throughout the seventies, if one harped on these values, one was dismissed as "living in the sixties." One is constantly being told that the purpose of life is to have fun. Perhaps for some people this is true. But as for me, give me *meaning* to my life and I exist. And don't get me wrong. I do not for one minute believe that homosexuals are intrinsically dishonest. It's just that from earliest consciousness, we are forced to be two-faced: certainly in the non-gay world of family and business and most definitely in the social gay world of posing and posturing. I think that surviving the gay social experience with a holistic sense about oneself gives one a survivor's sense of nobility. For whether it's the still strongly homophobic straight world or the strongly self-doubting gay world, there is a constant sense of struggle with visible and invisible demons for anyone who keeps his head above water. So finally, it was my sense of integrity which allowed me to present an ambivalent portrait of myself. Yet I do not like the idea of being disliked, even by strangers.

As to the specifics of the various insights presented in this book, I do not, as usual, accept the implications of some of Philip's major premises. He talks of my various "poses" as if they were distinct from some "real" me. I'm afraid that doesn't quite wash with me. A painting is, of course, viewed as a totality: not simply the tiny aspects that one likes on the canvas. Mona Lisa's smile couldn't exist without her dress. By the same token, me sitting in front of a microphone or standing on a pitcher's mound is no more or less real than my crying in Philip's arms or laying with him in quiet repose. I think what Philip is really saying is that he liked certain aspects of me and didn't like others. Period.

One of the conclusions he appears to have drawn is that I am "a Bohemian intellectual": a categorization which I find quite irritating. Perhaps the reason for my annoyance is that part of me has made strenuous attempts to be exactly like the prototypical "everyone else" for whom I generally have such utter contempt. Have you ever seen "so-and-so" walking down the street with his tee shirt and hair tucked in perfectly or her makeup on without a smudge. Well, I have made what at times were gargantuan efforts in that direction. But there was always a corner sticking out. Always a corner. And then of course, there has always been my one-two combination of mind to mouth which invariably comes up with the proverbial *Why. Why? Why? Why?*

Returning to the manuscript again and again, I realized that Philip was one of the few people who tended to out-why me. He is still a source of continued puzzlement to me. We speak daily on the phone and manage to see each other fortnightly in one context or another. But these settings are rarely our own abodes. We are both all too aware of the extremities of feelings that are underneath the genuine warmth we feel and express toward each other. I have also seen Philip become a man before my eyes, although he'll always retain vestiges of that youthful charm that I'm not sure I had even when I was a youth. He is still the man I would turn toward in a crowded room. But we don't deal with much anymore. But then every so often there is a twinge. Every so often there is a twinge of memory. Of croissants on the veranda in Cannes. Of Thanksgiving with Terry and Sally and the kids in Provincetown. Of appealing to our extraordinarily insightful friend Susan to adjudicate a dispute. Of some panel we spoke at on relationships with Betty and Ginny. Of running into Philip at a disco a year after he moved, dancing with him for the first time, and finding that we fit perfectly. Of making love at those special times. Of attempting to make love after the split. And finally, of smelling his odor any time I have been near him and remembering that odor long after he has gone. And yet for all of the ambivalent feelings that his presence draws from me, I can look at myself and say in all due honesty that I have loved, I do love and I will always love. So finally, it is those lovers who have survived for whom this book has been done and for those who haven't but who still *believe* that this is postscripted and dedicated.

Interviewing Lovers

It is difficult to speak the truth, for although there is only one truth, it is alive and therefore has a live and changing face.

—KAFKA

Generally speaking, it is inhumane to detain a fleeting insight.

—FRAN LEBOWITZ

INTERVIEWING

A N interview floats in clouds of ambiguity. Neither a portrait of someone by someone else nor a deliberate self-presentation, the interview arises out of the interaction between the interviewer and the interviewee. Thus the question of authorship is perplexing. In plain fact, no one *wrote* these interviews; three people *did* them. If several different people interviewed Philip and Neil, the result would be different interviews. Even if the same person interviewed Philip and Neil at different times, the result would be different interviews. So what makes any one interview better than another? Put it another way. What claim to serious consideration does an interview make?

"Words are formed by the tongue in the mouth," as Sartre once said, and an interview consists of spoken words. Are the words true? Who knows? Certainly the interviewer can't tell, unless he uses polygraph equipment. And the reader finds himself in an even worse position to judge their truth. The most you could say is that the story hangs together, doesn't contradict itself. But then neither does a good lie. Probability is the hallmark of fiction, more characteristic of it than of reality.

We do know that these words were spoken. By this person. At this time. Or on this occasion—the occasion being the question. ("Ask me a question. I don't know what to say when you don't ask me questions.") So an interview is a selection of moments when a voice spoke out. A selection because the moments were created by the questions. An interview is an attempt to make a particular moment of a particular person *there*, on the page, through the voice.

But the "voice" you "hear" on the page isn't the same as the voice electronically trapped on magnetic tape by my Sony. The printed words are a mere shadow of the original, full-bodied, living words "formed by the tongue in the mouth." The pitch, timbre, rhythm, loudness, texture, and silence have been lost— after all, how much can you do with italics, parentheses, dashes,

155

and dots? Furthermore, I've *edited* the transcripts. Diminished things that they were to begin with, I've cut them down to a small fraction of their original length. This selection, the editing, implicitly makes a claim—the claim that these words are worth listening to.

As far as I can see, that's the only claim an interview makes: that this is worth listening to. The interviews in this book certainly don't claim to be a definitive portrait of this concrete individual, Philip, or this concrete individual, Neil. Much less do they claim to be a portrait of that very elusive item, their love affair. Least of all do they pretend to be that most gossamer of all creatures, a portrait of a love affair (elusive) between two representative gay men (abstract)—we should leave such airy items to the social scientists in the wan hope that it keeps them off the streets.

These interviews do not present a love affair. They present two men talking about their love affair. That love was present to them while they were talking. But it wasn't there anymore. It was an absence they felt, like the ache you have when a tooth is gone. These interviews try to make present to the reader what was present to Philip and Neil by making Philip and Neil present to the reader.

The claim that this talk is worth listening to can only be tested by the reader. For my part, I feel quite comfortable in making it. I go around all the time telling people they should read that book or meet this person or see something or other. Which is fortunate, since I am by profession an editor. Of course, editors publish bombs, too. That's where the readers come in. To publish a book is to ask the public to make a judgment.

LOVERS

If the interview is a dubious form, the nature of love affairs is at least as problematical. There are two separate interviews in this book because there were two separate interpretations of the love affair, Philip's and Neil's. This is always the case with love affairs. But any interpretation is an interpretation of a "text." An interpretation is a perspective, and you can't have a perspective without having an object ("text") to perceive. It is precisely that "object" which is missing in love affairs, which is why lovers' quarrels are so murderous and maddening. There is no objective, common ground for mediation.

Love—romantic love or passion—seems to consist of nothing *but* perspective (the two-interpretations-and-no-text phenomenon). Love equals recognition. The lover is the only one who recognizes his beloved—which is why friends can never see what he sees in him. Someday Prince Charming will come along and recognize Cinderella for who she really is—his Princess. Some evening another Princess will kiss the toad, because she sees beneath his surface ugliness, and—poof!—he regains his real nature. The kiss that woke Sleeping Beauty was the kiss of recognition. Recognition and awakening, the lover and the beloved. For those passed over, Bette Midler wails, "You don't know me, you just don't know me." Love as passion, the mutual awakening and recognition of two lovers, is perhaps the greatest confirmation of our being we can experience. *I want you to be here. I want you to be you. You belong here, with me.* In our increasingly anonymous mass society it's no wonder that love overshadows all other themes of popular culture.

But love is a matter of feelings and a feeling is not a fact. A fact sits there, it stays the same. Two and two will always be four. It's a fact that the Germans invaded Belgium in August 1914. Facts have a stubborn irreducibility about them, which is both irritating and immensely reassuring. You can count on facts. But you can't count on feelings. Feelings not only change, they seem to *exist* in a state of flow. A feeling is more like a stream than like a pebble. It doesn't stay there, it goes on and in going on, it changes. This sounds pretty theoretical, but it has consequences.

Gays, because of their peculiar social situation, tend to try to build interpersonal relationships—love affairs—on their feelings alone. Without the subtle, numerous sanctions that usually support straight relationships, gay relationships tend to be grounded only on affectional preference, which is no ground at all but a vasty deep whose tides and currents are way beyond our ken, much less our control. Who understands why they love anyone? I can count the ways but not the reasons; you always end up with a *je ne sais quoi* or the banal idea that love is blind. It's because we don't love for any good reasons that love can never be deserved. I can owe respect, but not love. All of which does not bode well for lasting relationships. If love is beyond comprehension, it is even more beyond our control. I can promise to do something, but not to feel something. I can control, and thus predict, my behavior but not my feelings.

Which is not necessarily to be deplored. Among other things, it probably makes for our strongest connection with the wild, unpredictable, turbulent life of Nature. Now that the face of the earth has been overrun by man and Nature is on its way to being thoroughly domesticated, the passion of love may be our one remaining experience of the treacherous joy of Nature. It exacts a price, of course. But there's another side. Isak Dinesen found in Africa that she divided all creatures into the good (domestic) and the noble (wild); and while the good are useful, the noble, she felt, upheld the fierce dignity of creation.

And, of course, it would make gays the great romantics of our time.

In any event, these interviews suggested to me such thoughts about the problematical phenomenon of love—two sides but no coin. This elusive quality seemed to demand separate and independent interviews, a bifocal approach that might glimpse a three-dimensional but oddly insubstantial reality. The same desire for "bifocality" led to the use of photographs as well as the words generated in response to them. And again, it led to asking Philip and Neil to compose a written self-portrait in response to the verbal picture of them generated in the act of interviewing. If we have to have two sides but no coin, at least we could have two sides three times. So here you have it: the two sides of the story, the pictures and the words, the spoken and the written. In the space between these dualities, slipping through the interstices, something we call passion or love makes its presence felt. Like life, love remains an essential mystery. Talking about it is not an attempt to explain the mystery but to call attention to it.

M.D.